DISCARDED

Educational Standards

Affirmative Action
Amateur Athletics
American Military Policy
Animal Rights
Capital Punishment
DNA Evidence
Educational Standards
Election Reform
The FCC and Regulating Indecency
Fetal Rights
Freedom of Speech
Gay Rights
Gun Control
Immigrants' Rights After 9/11
Immigration Policy
Legalizing Marijuana
Mandatory Military Service
Media Bias
Mental Health Reform
Miranda Rights
Open Government
Physician-Assisted Suicide
Policing the Internet
Prisoners' Rights
Private Property Rights
Protecting Ideas
Religion in Public Schools
Rights of Students
The Right to Die
The Right to Privacy
Search and Seizure
Smoking Bans
Stem Cell Research and Cloning
Tort Reform
Trial of Juveniles as Adults
The War on Terror
Welfare Reform
Women in the Military

Educational Standards

David L. Hudson, Jr.

SERIES CONSULTING EDITOR
Alan Marzilli, M.A., J.D.

CHELSEA HOUSE PUBLISHERS
An imprint of Infobase Publishing

Educational Standards

Copyright © 2007 by Infobase Publishing

Chelsea House
An imprint of Infobase Publishing
132 West 31st Street
New York, NY 10001

Library of Congress Cataloging-in-Publication Data

Hudson, David L., 1969-
  Educational standards / David L. Hudson, Jr.
    p. cm. — (Point/counterpoint)
  Includes bibliographical references and index.
  ISBN-13: 978-0-7910-9278-1 (hardcover)
  ISBN-10: 0-7910-9278-X (hardcover)
  1. Education—Standards—United States—Juvenile literature. 2. Educational accountability—United States—Juvenile literature. 3. United States. No Child Left Behind Act of 2001—Juvenile literature. I. Title. II. Series.

  LB3060.83.H83 2007
  379.1'58—dc22   2007003601

Chelsea House books are available at special discounts when purchased in bulk quantities for businesses, associations, institutions, or sales promotions. Please call our Special Sales Department in New York at (212) 967-8800 or (800) 322-8755.

You can find Chelsea House on the World Wide Web at
http://www.chelseahouse.com

Series design by Keith Trego
Cover design by Takeshi Takahashi

Printed in the United States of America

Bang Hermitage 10 9 8 7 6 5 4 3 2 1

This book is printed on acid-free paper.

All links and Web addresses were checked and verified to be correct at the time of publication. Because of the dynamic nature of the Web, some addresses and links may have changed since publication and may no longer be valid.

CONTENTS

Foreword
Alan Marzilli, M.A., J.D.
Washington, D.C.

The debates presented in POINT/COUNTERPOINT are among the most interesting and controversial in contemporary American society, but studying them is more than an academic activity. They affect every citizen; they are the issues that today's leaders debate and tomorrow's will decide. The reader may one day play a central role in resolving them.

Why study both sides of the debate? It's possible that the reader will not yet have formed any opinion at all on the subject of this volume—but this is unlikely. It is more likely that the reader will already hold an opinion, probably a strong one, and very probably one formed without full exposure to the arguments of the other side. It is rare to hear an argument presented in a balanced way, and it is easy to form an opinion on too little information; these books will help to fill in the informational gaps that can never be avoided. More important, though, is the practical function of the series: Skillful argumentation requires a thorough knowledge of *both* sides—though there are seldom only two, and only by knowing what an opponent is likely to assert can one form an articulate response.

Perhaps more important is that listening to the other side sometimes helps one to see an opponent's arguments in a more human way. For example, Sister Helen Prejean, one of the nation's most visible opponents of capital punishment, has been deeply affected by her interactions with the families of murder victims. Seeing the families' grief and pain, she understands much better why people support the death penalty, and she is able to carry out her advocacy with a greater sensitivity to the needs and beliefs of those who do not agree with her. Her relativism, in turn, lends credibility to her work. Dismissing the other side of the argument as totally without merit can be too easy—it is far more useful to understand the nature of the controversy and the reasons *why* the issue defies resolution.

The most controversial issues of all are often those that center on a constitutional right. The Bill of Rights—the first ten amendments to the U.S. Constitution—spells out some of the most fundamental rights that distinguish the governmental system of the United States from those that allow fewer (or other) freedoms. But the sparsely worded document is open to interpretation, and clauses of only a few words are often at the heart of national debates. The Bill of Rights was meant to protect individual liberties; but the needs of some individuals clash with those of society as a whole, and when this happens someone has to decide where to draw the line. Thus the Constitution becomes a battleground between the rights of individuals to do as they please and the responsibility of the government to protect its citizens. The First Amendment's guarantee of "freedom of speech," for example, leads to a number of difficult questions. Some forms of expression, such as burning an American flag, lead to public outrage—but nevertheless are said to be protected by the First Amendment. Other types of expression that most people find objectionable, such as sexually explicit material involving children, are not protected because they are considered harmful. The question is not only where to draw the line, but how to do this without infringing on the personal liberties on which the United States was built.

The Bill of Rights raises many other questions about individual rights and the societal "good." Is a prayer before a high school football game an "establishment of religion" prohibited by the First Amendment? Does the Second Amendment's promise of "the right to bear arms" include concealed handguns? Is stopping and frisking someone standing on a corner known to be frequented by drug dealers a form of "unreasonable search and seizure" in violation of the Fourth Amendment? Although the nine-member U.S. Supreme Court has the ultimate authority in interpreting the Constitution, its answers do not always satisfy the public. When a group of nine people—sometimes by a five-to-four vote—makes a decision that affects the lives of hundreds of millions, public outcry can be expected. And the composition of the Court does change over time, so even a landmark decision is not guaranteed to stand forever. The limits of constitutional protection are always in flux.

These issues make headlines, divide courts, and decide elections. They are the questions most worthy of national debate, and this series aims to cover them as thoroughly as possible. Each volume sets out some of the key arguments surrounding a particular issue, even some views that most people consider extreme or radical—but presents a balanced perspective on the issue. Excerpts from the relevant laws and judicial opinions and references to central concepts, source material, and advocacy groups help the reader to explore the issues even further and to read "the letter of the law" just as the legislatures and the courts have established it.

It may seem that some debates—such as those over capital punishment and abortion, debates with a strong moral component—will never be resolved. But American history offers numerous examples of controversies that once seemed insurmountable but now are effectively settled, even if only on the surface. Abolitionists met with widespread resistance to their efforts to end slavery, and the controversy over that issue threatened to cleave the nation in two; but today public debate over the merits of slavery would be unthinkable, though racial inequalities still plague the nation. Similarly unthinkable at one time was suffrage for women and minorities, but this is now a matter of course. Distributing information about contraception once was a crime. Societies change, and attitudes change, and new questions of social justice are raised constantly while the old ones fade into irrelevancy.

Whatever the root of the controversy, the books in POINT/ COUNTERPOINT seek to explain to the reader the origins of the debate, the current state of the law, and the arguments on both sides. The goal of the series is to inform the reader about the issues facing not only American politicians, but all of the nation's citizens, and to encourage the reader to become more actively involved in resolving these debates, as a voter, a concerned citizen, a journalist, an activist, or an elected official. Democracy is based on education, and every voice counts—so every opinion must be an informed one.

As the global economy becomes more important, and the American economy moves further from farming and manufacturing into a service-based economy, perhaps nothing will define the nation's future so much as the education of young people. While almost everyone agrees that we must do a better job of educating children, particularly children of minority groups and those from low-income households, people disagree bitterly about the best ways to improve education. When President George W. Bush first ran for the White House in 2000, he and challenger Al Gore offered vastly different approaches to remedying failing schools and closing the achievement gap between schools serving mostly white students and those serving predominantly members of minority groups. While President Bush's legacy will probably be shaped largely by the Iraq conflict and the War on Terror, one of his most significant domestic policies has been the No Child Left Behind Act, a sweeping law requiring states to test and monitor students' achievement and offer alternatives to students in schools that do not measure up to state standards. The law has both its supporters and its critics, and this volume begins with an examination of their arguments. At the center of the federal law is standardized testing, which is used for purposes such as a prerequisite for advancing a grade or graduating. The volume looks at issues such as whether standardized testing narrows students' learning experience by forcing teachers to "teach to the test" and whether tests are culturally biased.

While much of the debate over educational standards is focused on "fixing" public education, some people believe that many schools are beyond repair and that alternatives are needed. Some of the alternatives include publicly-funded but privately-run charter schools, which can include schools run by for-profit companies, and providing students in failing public schools with vouchers that can be used to pay tuition at private schools, including religious schools. The controversies surrounding these issues are also explored in this volume.

Educational Standards

More than 50 years ago, U.S. Supreme Court Chief Justice Earl Warren wrote these eloquent words in the famous case that desegregated public schools, *Brown v. Board of Education*:

Today, education is perhaps the most important function of state and local governments. Compulsory school attendance laws and the great expenditures for education both demonstrate our recognition of the importance of education to our democratic society. It is required in the performance of our most basic public responsibilities, even service in the armed forces. It is the very foundation of good citizenship. Today it is a principal instrument in awakening the child to cultural values, in preparing him for later professional training, and in helping him to adjust normally to his environment. In these days, it is doubtful that any child may reasonably be expected to succeed in life if he is denied the opportunity of an education. Such an opportunity, where the state has undertaken to provide it, is a right which must be made available to all on equal terms.[1]

Warren emphasized the vital importance of education. Fifty years later, education remains "the most important function of state and local governments." It also remains the "principal instrument in awakening the child to cultural values." It is still true that those who receive a good education are far more likely to have a better quality of life than those who do not.

Because of the continued importance of education, it remains imperative that our children receive the best education possible. As President George W. Bush said in January 2002, "We owe the children of America a good education."[2] In school, children should learn the basic skills that they need to function well in later life. For this reason, it is important for educators, teachers, parents, students, and community leaders to ensure that the educational system is healthy. Community-wide standards are one way to accomplish that, but what those standards should be is not self-evident.

This book examines several controversial, high-profile debates in the education field. The first debate concerns perhaps the most controversial law to be passed in the area of education in the past 25 years. Its title conveys its importance: the No Child Left Behind Act (NCLB). The law introduces a new lexicon to the public, terms such as "adequate yearly progress," "highly qualified teachers," "proficient," and "school improvement plans." The law also has unleashed a torrential debate in which each side seems to engage in overstatement and exaggeration. Supporters claim that the law is an elixir that will cure the woes of public education. Detractors insist that the law is a weapon designed to destroy America's public schools. The reality lies somewhere in between these polar extremes.

To its supporters, the law ensures that all children will receive a quality education—that no child will be left behind. These supporters claim that the law instills greater accountability

The nation's education bill

President Bush signed the new education bill Tuesday with provisions for standardized tests and federal spending.

- Authorizes $26.5 billion for the 2002 budget year, which began Oct. 1, for K-12 education. That is about $8 billion more than the year before.

- Requires annual state tests in reading and math for every child in grades three through eight. Schools whose scores fail to improve two years in a row could receive more federal aid. If scores still fail to improve, low-income students can receive tutoring or transportation to another public school. A school in which scores fail to improve over six years could have staff changes.

- Allows churches or other religious groups to provide tutoring and after-school programs.

- Requires schools to raise all students to reading and math proficiency in the next 12 years. Schools also must close gaps between wealthy, poor students and white, minority students.

- Requires schools to ensure that within four years all teachers are qualified to teach in their subject area. If a teacher isn't qualified in a subject, a school would be required to send a letter notifying parents.

- Allows school districts to spend federal teacher-quality funds on training, hiring or teacher raises.

- Requires schools to develop periodic "report cards" showing a school's test scores compared with both local and state schools.

- Provides nearly $1 billion per year to help every student read by third grade.

- Requires schools to test students with limited English skills in English after three consecutive years of in a U.S. school.

SOURCE: Associated Press

AP

In 2002, President Bush signed into law the controversial No Child Left Behind Act, a federal education law that set specific goals for the coming decade. The graphic above summarizes some of the major provisions of the act.

in the educational system and that it provides the greatest assistance to minority children who for years have more often been the recipients of inferior educations.

In January 2006, on the fourth anniversary of the signing of No Child Left Behind, U.S. Secretary of Education Margaret Spellings announced that No Child Left Behind has been an undeniably positive force for the educational system. "The results are beginning to come in," Spellings said.

> They show a revival in mathematics achievement in the early grades, coupled with more reading progress in the past five years among nine-year-olds than in the previous three decades. Remarkable academic gains have been made by African American and Hispanic students, helping to close an achievement gap critics once called intractable and inevitable.[3]

Detractors of NCLB counter that the law is a federal invasion of local and state educational entities on an unprecedented scale. They contend that the law has done far more harm than good. To its detractors, NCLB represents the "perfect infernal machine to destroy public education in the United States."[4] They argue that NCLB reduces the curriculum because teachers teach to the tests and fail to give students a well-rounded education that includes history and the arts. They also contend that the law encourages states to lower their standards in order to ensure that more students pass the tests and avoid the punitive reach of the law.

The second major controversy covered in this book concerns the larger issue of standardized testing and standards-based reform in general. Students are tested more now than at any time in this nation's history. Supporters contend that standardized testing helps ensure that schools are accountable and are teaching our children. They point out that, despite the harsh rhetoric, standardized testing actually serves a very valuable purpose and is not designed to punish students. Rather, standardized testing serves as an important barometer of the educational system. These supporters also contend that the tests help prepare the students for the real world, where they will face numerous other tests and challenging experiences.

Critics counter that the nation's obsession with standardized testing has led to an undervaluing of real education. This process leads to what critic and author Peter Sacks has termed "standardized minds."[5] Critics assert that standardized tests do not accurately measure what students learn but rather test subjects in a superficial manner. They also argue that standardized tests discriminate against minority and lower-income students. These critics are particularly opposed to the so-called exit exams that can deny a passing student a diploma because of poor performance on a single test.

The third major source of controversy covered in this book focuses on the alternatives to traditional public schools. Most students in America are educated in the traditional arena of public schools. In recent years, however, alternative models have been proposed, given the perceived failure (critics and supporters disagree vehemently over whether public schools are failing) of some public schools. The response at the federal and state level has been to provide other educational options through school vouchers and charter schools.

Several members of both houses of Congress supported vouchers by introducing the America's Opportunity Scholarship for Kids Act.[6] This law would increase school choice for poorer students. Vouchers, which give money to parents who wish to send their children to non-public schools, and charter schools, a special type of public school that is exempt from traditional rules and regulations, offer increased educational opportunities, particularly for inner city children.

Critics argue that vouchers, charter schools, and the general move toward privatization of public education harm public schools by draining away critical resources, dividing students on religious grounds, and not living up to stated expectations. Some critics challenge that vouchers are part of the general move to destroy public education. Some also argue that voucher programs, many of which send students to private religious schools, violate the Establishment Clause of the First Amendment, which provides for separation of church and state.

These controversies show that the debate over educational standards remains as vital, vibrant, and, at times, vitriolic as ever. That is the essence of the American constitutional democracy: that citizens, politicians, students, teachers, and everyone else can vigorously debate and discuss important educational issues. This book hopes to contribute to that discussion.

No Child Left Behind Is a Positive Force for Improving Our Nation's Public Schools

There's no greater challenge than to make sure that every child—and all of us on this stage mean every child, not just a few children—every single child, regardless of where they live, how they're raised, the income level of their family, every child receives a first-class education in America.[7]

—President George W. Bush, January 8, 2002

O n January 8, 2002, President George W. Bush signed into law an ambitious education reform law called the No Child Left Behind Act (NCLB). The law, enacted with significant bipartisan support, cleared the House of Representatives by a vote of 381 to 41 and the Senate by 87 to 10. NCLB sets the laudable goal of requiring schools to ensure that nearly all students are proficient in the core subjects of English, math, and science. It seeks to ensure that no child in America is left behind—that every child, regardless of race, ethnicity, or wealth, receives a quality educa-

President Bush, seated, chats with a student as he signs the No Child Left Behind Act into law on January 8, 2002.

tion. Too often, poor and minority students do not receive the best education. NCLB is a historic piece of legislation that seeks to remedy that regrettable and uncomfortable reality.

The law creates accountability in our public school system. "The first principle is accountability," said President Bush. "Every school has a job to do. And that's to teach the basics and teach them well."[8] The law requires public schools across the country to test their students annually in grades 3 to 8 in reading and math. It also requires schools to test students in science once during each of the following grade groupings: 3 to 5, 6 to 9, and 10 to 12, by the 2007–2008 academic year. It requires states to establish their own standards and their own standardized tests, giving flexibility and not imposing a rigid, one-size-fits-all formula. The law requires schools to make "adequate yearly progress" with respect to student test scores. Schools also have to demonstrate that they are employing "high-quality" teachers. These various measures are designed to create a better public school system.

The law was not the product or brainchild of one political party. Many people identify NCLB as having been created by President Bush, but that is too simplistic. President Bush did play a large role in supporting the law and getting it passed, and he modeled his initial proposal on school reforms instituted in Texas while he was governor of that state; however, many Democratic members of Congress played key roles in various aspects of the law, which is more than 600 pages long. Longtime Democratic senator Edward Kennedy of Massachusetts was a prime supporter and sponsor of NCLB in 2001–2002. Another Democratic congressman, George Miller of California, played a key role in various provisions, particularly the teacher-quality provisions.[9]

NCLB continues an important commitment to improving education for our youth.

NCLB is often demonized as a wholesale federal intrusion into local educational matters. Teachers' unions, which oppose the "high-quality" teacher aspects of the law, vilify the law with its supposed "excessive focus on accountability based on standardized tests."[10] Some aspects of NCLB are different from prior federal legislation, but it is important to understand that NCLB is a natural progression of earlier efforts by the federal government to improve education. NCLB is not an anomalous beast; it is a more refined and comprehensive effort at educational reform that echoes the goals of prior legislation.

In 1965, Congress passed the Elementary and Secondary Education Act (ESEA), which sought to improve the education of lower-income schoolchildren. In the 1970s, Congress increased funding and spending for ESEA, sending more money into schools across the country. In the 1980s, however, many people became concerned that, despite increased funding, public schools were not fulfilling their important mission. In 1983, the National Commission on Excellence in Education issued an influential report titled *A Nation at Risk: The Imperative for Educational Reform.*[11] In its recommendations, the commission urged that schools commit to better instruction in "the five new basics," including greater learning in English, mathematics, and science. Another recommendation was that "standardized tests of

President George W. Bush on No Child Left Behind

To keep this country prosperous and to keep this country hopeful, we've got to make sure these public schools of ours stay strong, and we started on that road to strengthening every public school three years ago, when I signed the No Child Left Behind Act. The theory of this law is straightforward, it's pretty easy to understand: that in return for federal dollars, we are asking for results. That makes sense if you're a taxpayer. It makes sense, frankly, if you're an innovative teacher and a strong principal. We're leaving behind the old attitude that it's okay for some students just to be shuffled through the system. That's not okay. And three years ago we began to change the system that too often had given up on a child, primarily those children whose mothers or dads didn't speak English as a first language or those children who may be growing up in inner-city America, whose mom or dad didn't have big income levels. This administration believes, and most people in America believe that every child can learn.

And so we're raising the standards for every public school in America. If you believe every child can learn, then it makes sense to raise the bar, not lower the bar. If you believe every child can learn, then it makes sense to measure to determine whether every child is learning. That's called accountability, accountability for results. Accountability is so crucial to achieve our goal for every child learning to read, write, add and subtract. Accountability helps to correct problems early, before it is too late. Accountability enables a good teacher to test a curriculum as to whether or not that curriculum is working. Accountability allows principals and teachers to determine whether methodology is working. Accountability also is a way to make sure parents stay involved in the educational systems across our country.

Source: "President Discusses No Child Left Behind and High School Initiatives," January 12, 2005, http://www.whitehouse.gov/news/releases/2005/01/20050112-5.html.

achievement (not to be confused with aptitude tests) should be administered at major transition points from one level of schooling to another."[12]

NCLB simply is the latest and greatest attempt by the federal government to follow these recommendations and to encourage schools to provide better instruction and learning in the core areas of English, math, and science. It attempts to implement *The Nation at Risk* recommendation for greater use of "standardized testing" to ensure that students are actually learning in school.

In 1994, President Bill Clinton and Congress approved a law called Goals 2000: Educate America Act. This law, which was a

Definition: "Adequate Yearly Progress"

"Adequate yearly progress" shall be defined by the State in a manner that—
  (i) applies the same high standards of academic achievement to all public elementary school and secondary school students in the State;
  (ii) is statistically valid and reliable;
  (iii) results in continuous and substantial academic improvement for all students;
  (iv) measures the progress of public elementary schools, secondary schools and local educational agencies and the State based primarily on the academic assessments described in paragraph (3);
  (v) includes separate measurable annual objectives for continuous and substantial improvement for each of the following:
    (I) The achievement of all public elementary school and secondary school students.
    (II) The achievement of—
      (aa) economically disadvantaged students;
      (bb) students from major racial and ethnic groups;
      (cc) students with disabilities; and
      (dd) students with limited English proficiency;

Source: Section 1111 of No Child Left Behind Act, http://www.ed.gov/policy/elsec/leg/esea02/pg2.html#sec1111.

reauthorization of the 1965 ESEA, required all public schools to create standardized tests that would make the schools accountable. One of the stated legislative goals was that "United States students will be first in the world in mathematics and science achievement." In some ways, NCLB simply reflects the federal government's continued commitment to education begun with ESEA, *The Nation at Risk*, and Goals 2000: The Educate America Act.

NCLB is proving effective in addressing the achievement gap.

Title I of the No Child Left Behind Act is called "Improving the Academic Achievement of the Disadvantaged." A primary purpose behind NCLB was to bridge the gap between African-American and Latino students on the one hand and white and Asian students on the other. For far too long, African-American, Latino, and poor students of all races have lagged behind others in school achievement. Much of this has been because these students have not had the same opportunities and quality of education. Educational opportunities are a key predictor of future success, and many of these students have not had a fair chance. NCLB seeks to change this culture and broaden the scope of opportunities for underperforming and disadvantaged children. The law forces school districts to account for the performance of all students and requires schools to examine the performance of students in different categories.

NCLB requires schools to report the standardized test results of all their students. The law also makes the schools disaggregate—or separate—these data and report the results of different student subgroups. This means that schools must report the test results of different racial groups, low-income students, students with disabilities, and so-called limited English students. By requiring schools to separate the data, the law forces them to come up with ways to help all students improve.

New York City Schools Chancellor Joel Klein supports the NCLB in large part because it attempts to close the alarming achievement gap based on race. "When they passed NCLB,

No Child Left Behind and Accountability

Accountability is a crucial step in addressing the achievement gaps that plague our nation. For too long, the poor achievement of our most vulnerable students has been lost in unrepresentative averages. African-American, Hispanic, special education, limited English proficient, and many other students were left behind because schools were not held accountable for their individual progress. Now all students count.

Under No Child Left Behind, every state is required to 1) set standards for grade-level achievement and 2) develop a system to measure the progress of all students and subgroups of students in meeting those state-determined grade-level standards.

Source: U.S. Department of Education, *A Guide to Education and No Child Left Behind*, 2004, http://www.ed.gov/nclb/overview/intro/guide/index.html.

our national leaders finally took responsibility for the fact that white and Asian students are performing four years ahead of African-American and Latino students in high school," he said in a May 2006 speech in Connecticut. "Four years. And this law finally put muscle behind the attempt to close that gap."[13] President Bush has mentioned the "soft bigotry of low expectations." He means that school officials must accept nothing short of achievement from all students and high-quality educational services in all school districts. Columnist Ruben Navarrette Jr. said it well: "There is racism here, but not in the law [NCLB]. Rather, it is built into the educational system that the law seeks to reform."[14]

Application of the law is starting to show some positive results. In Minnesota, the percent of African-American fifth graders scoring proficiently in math doubled between 2000 and 2005, and in Illinois, Latino fifth graders have also improved dramatically on their math tests. In both of these examples, the achievement gap has narrowed dramatically.[15]

NCLB gives parents the needed flexibility to obtain a good education for their children.

NCLB leaves options for parents with children at underperforming schools. The law allows parents to make individual decisions to have their child moved to a better school. If a school has underperformed and has not made "adequate yearly progress," then the school district must provide parents the option of having their child transferred to a school that is performing properly. "Any school that doesn't perform, any school that cannot catch up and do its job, a parent will have these options—a better public school, a tutor, or a charter school," President Bush said when signing the measure. "We do not want children trapped in schools that will not change and will not teach."

Congress included this aspect of NCLB because many members thought it was unfair to label schools as failing without providing an option for children to attend a better school. Some legislators also hoped that the transfer option would create

Definition: "Highly Qualified" Teacher Provision

HIGHLY QUALIFIED–The term 'highly qualified'—
  (A) when used with respect to any public elementary school or secondary school teacher teaching in a State, means that—
    (i) the teacher has obtained full State certification as a teacher (including certification obtained through alternative routes to certification) or passed the State teacher licensing examination, and holds a license to teach in such State, except that when used with respect to any teacher teaching in a public charter school, the term means that the teacher meets the requirements set forth in the State's public charter school law; and
    (ii) the teacher has not had certification or licensure requirements waived on an emergency, temporary, or provisional basis.

Source: Title IX of NCLB, http://www.ed.gov/policy/elsec/leg/esea02/pg107.html.

greater incentives for underperforming schools to improve their performance.[16] NCLB also allows greater penalties to be imposed on school districts that continually fail to make adequate yearly progress. If a school fails for four straight years, then the state must take more drastic actions, such as replacing school staff. If a school continues to fail, then the state may take control of the school and reorganize it under private management, as a charter school, or under completely new leadership. These may seem like drastic remedies, but the goal is vitally important. Americans do not want students placed in failing schools.

U.S. Secretary of Education Margaret Spellings testified before the House Education Committee in September 2005: "We've made more progress in the last 5 years than in the previous 30 combined." The reason for the increased progress is that NCLB provides the needed enforcement to ensure positive results.

NCLB recognizes the importance of teacher quality.

NCLB requires that children be taught by "highly qualified teachers." Some experts believe that this is one of the more

Kati Haycock, Director of the Education Trust

The teacher quality provisions in NCLB embody three basic principles:

> First, all students are entitled to qualified teachers who know their subjects. Second, parents deserve information on their children's teachers and the qualifications of teachers in their schools. Finally, NCLB recognizes that states, school districts and the national government have a special responsibility to ensure that poor and minority students get their fair share of qualified, experienced teachers.

Source: Testimony Before the House Committee on Education and the Workforce, http://edworkforce.house.gov/hearings/109th/fc/spellingsnclb092905/haycock.htm.

"significant departure[s]" from existing federal law.[17] Under this provision, every state must take steps to ensure that every student has a "highly qualified" teacher. Traditionally, poorer urban and rural school districts have had trouble obtaining and retaining teachers. This represents a challenge to the educational system's goal of providing a good education to all children. If children do not have competent teachers providing good instruction, they can be left behind. As the result of an effort spearheaded by one of NCLB's original authors, Representative George Miller (D.-Cal.), the law includes the "highly qualified" teacher requirement.

In a July 2006 report, the Citizens Commission on Civil Rights called teacher quality "a paramount civil rights issue for school children in this century."[18] Teachers represent the lifeblood of the classrooms: They are primarily responsible for the education of the nation's youth. Studies have shown that students taught by effective teachers are likely to outperform students who are not.[19] NCLB seeks to ensure that all students—especially students in poorer rural and urban school districts—are not shortchanged and that they, too, will have the tools to achieve in society. One way to guarantee this opportunity is to ensure that students' teachers are qualified in the subjects that they teach. Sandra Feldman, a former president of the American Federation of Teachers, said at a White House conference meeting in 2001, "You can't teach what you don't know well."[20]

Summary

NCLB is a misunderstood law that has been vilified in certain circles. But NCLB is not the problem. Rather, it is an important attempt to improve the quality of education in our nation's schools. NCLB is also the culmination of years of concern about the performance of schools. Often, improvement does not occur

U.S. Secretary of Education Margaret Spellings

Clearly, we are on the right track. The law is working. . . .

No Child Left Behind is provoking a lot of discussion about how we can best help the most students. We are learning from our experiences and from the research as it develops. Our ongoing conversations about remaining issues are right and appropriate. If this Act had not become law, I'm not sure we would be having these conversations.

Before No Child Left Behind, students were too often shuffled from grade to grade without knowing how to read or do math. It's right and righteous that the law focused on these two key areas. The next step is to take high standards and accountability into our high schools. . . .

With No Child Left Behind, President Bush and you in the Congress led our nation in an historic commitment to give every child a quality education. We looked ourselves in the mirror and said we would close the achievement gap by 2014 . . . across the board.

It's our mission, and it's also the right thing to do. Our children and our country deserve no less.

Source: Statement to House Committee on Education and the Workforce, September 29, 2005, http://edworkforce.house.gov/hearings/109th/fc/spellingsnclb092905/spellings.htm.

without accountability. There is nothing wrong with holding schools accountable for teaching children—all children.

NCLB seeks to continue the federal government's role as overseer of education, to close the alarming achievement gap in American schools, and to improve teacher quality. There is nothing wrong with these lofty goals. Our nation's children deserve no less than full commitment. That is the essence of the No Child Left Behind Act, a flexible response to a serious issue.

Secretary Spellings is correct. No Child Left Behind is a monumentally important piece of legislation necessary to improve the American educational system. As she said, "Our children and our country deserve no less."

No Child Left Behind Is a Misguided Law That Does More Harm Than Good

> The biggest problem with the NCLB Act is that it mistakes measuring schools for fixing them.[21]
>
> —Linda Darling-Hammond,
> Professor of Education, Stanford University

Susan Ohanian, a teacher for many years, speaks across the country at conferences to urge teachers to oppose No Child Left Behind. She seeks to raise awareness of a law that is up for reauthorization in 2007 and to help gather one million signatures in an effort that she calls the "resistance movement" to combat No Child Left Behind. "There comes a time when you can't participate in a system that's harming children," she recently said at the annual conference of the National Council of Teachers of English in Nashville, Tennessee.[22] Ohanian fervently believes that NCLB does far more harm than good to the public educational system.

The law is called No Child Left Behind, but many in the education field refer to it by other less complimentary names, including "No Child Left Untested" and "No School Board Left Standing."[23] The law encourages states to lower their educational standards, imposes a one-size-fits-all testing requirement on school districts, hurts the schools and children that it was designed to help most, and suffers from woeful underfunding. It drives teachers away from poorer school districts, increases the marginalization of at-risk children, and moves schools away from teaching subjects other than reading and math. No Child Left Behind sounds like a good policy, but in reality is an unmitigated disaster. It has led to massive complaints from the educational community and a growing number of lawsuits from the states. Congress needs to take a serious look at this law when it is up for reauthorization in 2007.

NCLB encourages states to lower their standards.

No Child Left Behind requires schools to meet state educational standards in reading and math for the stated purpose of ensur-

Stan Karp

In general, the massive increase in testing that NCLB will impose on schools will hurt their educational performances, not improve them. When schools become obsessed with test scores, they narrow the focus of what teachers do in classrooms and limit their ability to serve the broader needs of children and their communities.

Source: Stan Karp, "NCLB's Selective Vision of Equality: Some Gaps Count More Than Others," in *Many Children Left Behind*, ed. Deborah Meier and George Wood. Boston: Beacon Press, 2004.

ing that all children receive a quality education. The act's goals are minimized, however, because the law allows the states to set their own educational standards. Legal commentator James E. Ryan wrote that "the Act's fatal flaw is that it creates incentives that work against the Act's goals."[24] He explained that "while it [the act] is supposed to raise academic achievement across all schools, it creates incentives for states to lower academic standards."[25]

The act contains such "perverse" incentives because it imposes severe penalties on schools that fail to make "adequate yearly progress" on student test scores. Many states have responded to this federal law by lowering their standards, sparing their schools from federal penalties. According to education commentator Linda Darling-Hammond, "One of the first perverse consequences of the NCLB Act is that many states formally lowered their standards in order to avoid having most of their schools declared failing."[26]

The problem is that the law imposes harsh penalties on schools for failing to make "adequate yearly progress" in a variety of areas. The penalties become progressively more severe, up to the closing of schools and hiring new management, or remanagement, for schools that fail for five or more consecutive years. ("Remanagement" means that the state takes over and manages the school or assigns another entity to manage the school; in other words, the current leadership is out.) School districts obviously do not wish to face these harsh penalties; therefore, the states have a strong incentive to lower the educational standards to ensure that more schools meet them.

NCLB reduces the quality of schools' curricula by focusing too much on reading and math.

NCLB requires standardized testing for students in the core subjects of math and reading, and it measures schools' progress based on the results of these standardized tests. This means that schools are devoting more and more time to teach to the tests—

Testing to become the standard

Under the No Child Left Behind Act, schools during the 2005-06 academic year will be required to test their students in reading and math every year from third through eighth grade. Standardized testing at every grade is in place in only about half the states.

States that need to develop at least 10 tests

D.C.

SOURCE: Education Commission of the States   AP

Under the No Child Left Behind Act, schools are required to test students in grades 3 to 8 in reading and math every year; the testing was to be in place for the 2005–2006 academic year. As of May 2005, as the graphic above shows, only half of the states had such testing in place.

that is, designing lessons to mirror the content on the tests—to make sure that their students score adequately. There is nothing wrong with solid instruction in reading and math, but this focus has led to a phenomenon known as "narrowing the curriculum." The National Council for the Social Studies testified before the U.S. House of Representatives Committee on Education and the Workforce in May 2006: "It is obvious that the potential narrowing of the curriculum as an inadvertent consequence of the implementation of NCLB warrants the attention of educators and policymakers across the nation."[27]

Schools have cut into music appreciation, physical education, social studies, and various other subjects in order to devote more time to reading and math. Schools hope such changes will ensure higher tests scores in reading and math. "The intense focus on the two basic skills is a sea change in American instructional practice, with many schools that once offered rich curriculums now systematically trimming courses like social studies, science and art," Sam Dillon wrote in the *New York Times.*[28]

The Center on Education Policy, an independent think tank devoted to improving education, conducted a survey (released in 2005) that showed that many school districts were engaged in the practice of narrowing the curriculum. The findings showed that 27 percent of the schools surveyed reported that they had somewhat or significantly reduced social studies teaching in order to focus more on preparing students for the standardized math and reading tests. Another 22 percent of schools reduced instruction in science in order to provide more reading and math instruction.[29] A later survey by the Center on Education Policy found that 71 percent of surveyed school districts had reduced instruction in at least one area to make room for more math and reading testing. The report recommended that "the Secretary of Education should use her bully pulpit to signal that social studies, science, the arts, and other subjects beside reading and math are still a vital part of a balanced curriculum."[30]

Because of this narrowing of the curriculum, many educational organizations are calling for a major overhaul or revision of NCLB. The National Council for the Social Studies and more than 80 other organizations signed a statement that advocates change in part because NCLB has led to "narrowing curriculum and instruction to focus on test preparation rather than richer academic learning."[31]

Social studies prepares students to become acquainted with civic life, participation in politics, and major issues that govern the world. If students are not taught social studies, they will not be equipped with the tools to understand the world around them. NCLB threatens citizenship training by undervaluing social studies and overfocusing on standardized math and reading tests.[32]

NCLB is destined for failure because it is underfunded.

NCLB did receive bipartisan support and contains some important and even laudable goals. Unfortunately, the federal government has failed to provide the necessary funding to ensure that the act will serve its high purposes. The fundamental problem is that schools are not equally funded. The U.S. Supreme Court ruled in *San Antonio Independent School District v. Rodriguez* (1973) that there was no constitutional violation for schools to be funded by local property taxes.[33] "It has simply never been within the constitutional prerogative of this Court to nullify statewide measures for financing public services merely because the burdens or benefits thereof fall unevenly depending upon the relative wealth of the political subdivisions in which citizens live," the Court majority wrote.[34] The result of the *Rodriguez* decision is that students who attend schools in poorer districts,

Senator Edward Kennedy

We recognized when the law was passed that resources would be critical to carry the bold plan to leave no child behind to every school in America, and Congress promised significant increases in funding each year to get the job done. Unfortunately, President Bush still doesn't realize that No Child Left Behind was a promise, not a political slogan.

Over the past four years, the White House and this Republican Congress have shortchanged funding for the law to the tune of $40 billion.

Source: Statement of Senator Edward Kennedy, January 9, 2006, http://www.tedkennedy.com/journal/572/kennedy-on-no-child-left-behind-four-years-later.

with less tax revenue to fund education, simply don't have the same learning opportunities that students in wealthier districts have. This disparity in finances between school districts is the reality of American public school education. NCLB exacerbates this problem by imposing a one-size-fits-all mandate on schools with vastly different resources. The net effect is a situation in which poorer school districts are earmarked for failure while wealthier school districts are far more likely to meet the standards.

The only way for NCLB to live up to its lofty goals is for the government to provide greater financial resources to schools that desperately need such assistance. NCLB is not properly funded and, thus, will lead to an even greater divide between rich and poor school districts.

Lawsuits have been filed in several states to challenge aspects of NCLB with regard to funding. In August 2005, in *Connecticut v. Spellings,* the state of Connecticut sued the federal government over NCLB's so-called Unfunded Mandate Provision. This provision states:

> Nothing in this chapter shall be construed to authorize an officer or employee of the Federal Government to mandate, direct, or control a State, local educational agency, or school's curriculum, program of instruction, or allocation of State or local resources, or mandate a State or any subdivision thereof to spend any funds or incur any costs not paid for under this chapter.

The lawsuit alleges that Secretary of Education Spellings's "rigid enforcement of the NCLB Act's every grade testing requirement will compel Connecticut to spend millions of dollars over and above the federal funds in order to satisfy the NCLB every grade testing mandate."

In effect, the federal government requires all sorts of state testing but then fails to provide the financial backing for such an onerous, or burdensome, undertaking. The state of Connecticut contends that NCLB is violating its own "unfunded mandate provision" and the Tenth Amendment to the U.S. Constitution, and exceeds the U.S. Congress's powers under the Spending Clause of the Constitution. The unfunded mandate provision potentially violates the Tenth Amendment, which reserves many governmental powers for state governments to handle, because it represents federal infringement of state authority. "No matter how good its goals—and I agree with NCLB's goals—the federal government is not above the law," said Connecticut attorney general Richard Blumenthal. "The goals of the No Child Left Behind Act are laudable—indeed, Connecticut has pursued these goals for decades—but the federal government has failed in implementing them. Unfunded mandates are all too common; these specific unfunded mandates are unlawful."[35]

Other suits have been filed in Michigan and Arizona to challenge parts of NCLB. The lawsuit in Michigan, *Pontiac v. Spellings*, is spearheaded by the teachers' union, the National Education Association (NEA). The NEA believes that Congress

Connecticut Attorney General Richard Blumenthal

Our message to federal officials: Give up your unfunded mandates or give us the money. Live up to the law's promise. Show us flexibility or show us the money. We begin this federal court battle today—before spending one cent on illegal unfunded mandates this fiscal year. Hundreds of millions of dollars are at stake. Again and again, in letters and meetings, the federal government has rejected our repeated waiver requests unreasonably and arbitrarily. This mindless rigidity harms our taxpayers, but most of all, our children, who are robbed of resources in their classrooms. We will not dumb down our tests—as the federal education officials suggested—or divert money from critical existing educational programs.

Source: Press Release, Connecticut Attorney General's Office, August 22, 2005, http://www.ct.gov/ag/cwp/view.asp?A=1949&Q=300456.

has failed to fulfill its funding promises under NCLB: "The truth is that the administration and Congress have not provided enough funding and support for schools to follow the testing regimen and other regulations in the law."[36] Arizona has sued the federal government over NCLB because the federal law requires schools to include the test scores of children with fewer than three years of English instruction in its academic progress reports. The state of Arizona countered that schools should not be considered failing based on the test scores of students who haven't had enough time to master the English language. "I believe in testing in English," said Arizona school superintendent Tom Horne, "I just think you need to give the kids enough time to test proficiently on the test in English."[37]

Some members of Congress are urging their colleagues to modify NCLB to ensure proper funding. In January 2005, Representative Chris Van Hollen (D.-Md.) introduced the Keep Our Promise to America's Children and Teachers Act or the "Keep Our PACT Act."[38] This bill would require full funding of NCLB. "It's time to keep our promises to the children of America," said Van Hollen. "Over the years, there's been lots of talk about giving schoolchildren the resources they need to succeed; now it is time for reality to match the rhetoric. We need to send a message right now to our children and future generations that we will give them our full support."[39]

Summary

Many members of Congress recognize that NCLB needs to be modified or even overhauled. In April 2005, Representative Rosa DeLauro (D.-Conn.) introduced the No Child Left Behind Reform Act in the House, and Senator Chris Dodd (D.-Conn.) introduced a similar measure in the Senate.[40] These measures would give schools additional flexibility in showing that they have made adequate yearly progress and additional ways to show that their teachers are "highly qualified." The legislation would also provide for greater funding.

At least some of the stated goals of NCLB are noble and laudable. Most Americans certainly want to close the achievement gap between different races of students and reduce inequities of education that are based on wealth. Most schools certainly do not want to leave any child behind. The path to improving public schools, however, does not lie in imposing punitive measures on inner-city and rural schools that are most likely to fail to meet the standardized test requirements. Standardized tests are not the ultimate measure of school performance. NCLB results in narrowing the curriculum, lessening the quality of education overall, and undervaluing at-risk children. Furthermore, the federal government has invaded the province of state and local educational matters without providing adequate funding. No Child Left Behind needs major changes or it will continue to wreak havoc on the American educational system.

Standardized Testing Motivates Students and Creates Accountability in Schools

I n the early 1980s, Dennis Kennedy was a star linebacker for Judson High School in Converse, Texas. He played well enough on the football field to earn a scholarship to the University of Houston. The problem was that, according to Kennedy, he managed to graduate from high school even though he could barely read or write. He has said that he often cheated his way through high school. It hurt him in college, where he failed one English course three times. Kennedy managed to overcome his reading deficiencies through hard work and dedication, and now he teaches a course on business and society at the College of Business at the University of Texas at San Antonio.[41]

Unfortunately, Dennis Kennedy's story is not unique. Former NFL great Dexter Manley admitted that he managed to graduate from high school, attend college, and make it to the NFL even though he was illiterate. Perhaps Dennis Kennedy and

Dexter Manley would not have been passed through the educational system if they had been forced to take more rigorous standardized tests to measure what they were learning.

Standardized testing performs a vital function in the public school system by showing that students are learning in schools. Such tests give parents the knowledge that their children are learning the basic materials that they need to succeed later in life. Equally important, standardized tests ensure accountability in schools. If students continue to perform poorly on standardized tests, something needs to change. School officials should not warehouse (that is, keep students enrolled without making efforts to educate them) poorly performing students until they drop out; rather, schools should identify underperforming students and seek to raise their performance levels.

To read the popular press, one would think that standardized tests are a discriminatory waste of time that serve no important purposes. Nothing could be further from the truth. In reality, standardizing testing provides the best possible way to measure student performance in order to understand how schools can function better. There is no way to improve the public school system if educators and legislators do not know what needs to be fixed.

As with many areas, standardized testing has its own language or jargon. Much of the literature—both pro and con—in the area of standardized testing requires a basic understanding of key terms. Two of these terms are "norm-referenced tests" and "criterion-related tests." A norm-referenced test compares a student's performance on tests to how well other students performed. If a student scored in the eighty-fifth percentile, he scored better than 85 percent of students in the national norm for the test. A criterion-related test does not compare students' scores with others' but rather compares their scores to a critical mass of knowledge. Many believe that it is more important to determine what students learned than how they compare with others. For this reason, criterion-related tests are more popular.[42]

Another important concept in the area of standardized testing concerns tests called "high-stakes testing." This refers to tests that have important positive or negative consequences.[43] The previous two chapters showed that No Child Left Behind requires states to have more high-stakes tests. This is done to ensure that students are learning the basics in reading, math, and science. There are other forms of high-stakes testing in schools: Many states now require students to pass some sort of exit exam before they can obtain their diploma. This means that students must achieve a certain score on the test to obtain their diplomas.

Much criticism of standardized testing is simply not well founded.

Tests are blamed for many woes in the educational system, and they are the target of fierce criticism. Much of this criticism is undeserved. Professor and test creator Stephen G. Sireci wrote, "standardized tests have a bad reputation but that is an undeserved one."[44] He explained:

> People accused standardized tests of being unfair, biased, and discriminatory. Believe it or not, standardized tests are actually designed to promote test fairness. Standardized simply means that the test content is equivalent across administrations and that the conditions under which the test is administered are the same for all test takers. Thus, standardized tests are designed to provide a level playing field. That is, all test takers are given the same test under the same conditions.[45]

Some critics have alleged that standardized tests discriminate against minority students and students from low-income families. This is not true. Many states have utilized special bias review committees to ensure that the tests are fair and not biased against any group of students.[46]

Critics of standardized testing insist that members of the educational system despise these tests. Some educators may dislike standardized tests, but many polls have shown that parents support those tests. They want their children to learn and achieve more. Education expert Richard Phelps wrote that "low-income parents are often stronger supporters of high-stakes testing than higher income parents."[47] A recent poll among parents in California provided strong evidence that 80 percent of Latino parents and 68 percent of African-American parents support the state's standardized testing regime.[48]

The civil rights group Education Trust-West, based in Oakland, California, supports the exit exam in California. The group's director, Russlynn Ali, said that she and her colleagues have been called "sell outs" for supporting the exit exam, which requires students to pass a test in order to receive their diploma. She explained that these criticisms are unfounded and she pointed out that the standardized test is a step in the right direction because it is "beginning to level the playing field."[49]

Standardized tests do not violate constitutional or statutory rights.

Through the years, plaintiffs have raised a host of legal challenges to standardized tests. Some plaintiffs have alleged that standardized tests violate due process rights because they infringe on a student's property interest in education (that is, a student has a "property interest" in a diploma) without providing sufficient notice. Others allege that standardized tests violate equal protection because they discriminate against minorities. Still others contend that some standardized tests violate a federal law known as Title VI of the Civil Rights Act of 1964, which prohibits discrimination based on race, color, or national origin in any program that receives federal funding. Critics charge that standardized tests used in public educational systems violate Title VI because they negatively affect minorities more than other students.

When critics first began disputing the value of standardized testing, a few challenges were successful. In *Debra P. v. Turlington*, a federal appeals court determined that a standardized test in the state of Florida that students needed to pass to obtain their diploma violated their rights to due process because the students were not given sufficient notice that they had to pass the test to earn their diplomas.[50] The court also determined that the tests did not actually test what students were learning. That case was decided in 1981, however, more than 25 years ago. Standardized tests are much better now, and students are given sufficient notice of the effect of their test scores.

Recent court decisions establish that standardized testing requirements—even those that carry important consequences— do not violate constitutional or statutory rights. In *GI Forum Image De Tejas v. Texas Educ. Agency*, a federal court in Texas ruled that the Texas Assessment of Academic Skills examination, a test that students must pass before they obtain their diplomas, is constitutional.[51] The plaintiffs contended that the test violated Title VI because it worked a disparate impact on minorities—that is, it treated minorities differently, which could have an adverse effect on their scores and education. The court found otherwise, determining that the test was given in order to try to improve the educational system for all students.

FROM THE BENCH

GI Forum Image De Tejas v. Texas Educ. Agency, 87 F.Supp.2d 667, 670 (W.D. Tex. 2000)

In other words, the Plaintiffs were required to prove, by a preponderance of the evidence, that the TAAS test was implemented in spite of the disparities or that the TAAS test has perpetuated the disparities, and that requiring passage of the test for graduation is therefore fundamentally unfair. The Court believes that this has not been proven. Instead, the evidence suggests that the State of Texas was aware of probable disparities and that it designed the TAAS accountability system to reflect an insistence on standards and educational policies that are uniform from school to school.

The plaintiffs pressed their argument that the tests worked a disparate impact on minority students. The court concluded, however, that the plaintiffs failed to prove that any adverse impacts of the tests were "more significant" than the positive impact of the tests. The court concluded, "In the absence of such proof, the State must be allowed to design an educational system that it believes best meets the need of its citizens."[52]

The evidence in the case established that Hispanic and African-American students performed "significantly worse" on the Texas standardized test; however, it also established the "highly significant" fact that "minority students have continued to narrow the passage rate gap at a rapid rate."[53] The test may have a disparate impact on certain minority students, but the court determined that the test served the "legitimate educational purposes" of the state: "to hold schools, students and teachers accountable for education and to ensure that all Texas students receive the same, adequate learning opportunities."[54] According to the court, the test "accomplishes what it sets out to accomplish, which is to provide an objective assessment of whether students have mastered a discrete set of skills and knowledge."[55] The court also noted that the challengers to the test failed to present a satisfactory alternative that would provide the same type of "systemic accountability" in the educational system.

An Indiana appeals court reached a similar decision when it upheld the state's Graduation Qualifying Examination, which required all students to pass a standardized test to advance and graduate.[56] A group of disabled students, who had previously received exemptions from standardized tests, challenged the requirement on due process grounds. The court rejected this argument, pointing out that the students had at least three years' notice that they would have to take such an exam.

The disabled students also argued that the testing requirement violated a federal law known as the Individuals with Disabilities Education Act, or IDEA, which requires states that receive federal funds to offer special education programs and services in conjunction with individualized educational programs developed for the disabled children. The court noted that IDEA does not mandate certain results but provides disabled students access to certain programs. The state of Indiana did not deny access to educational programs when it imposed a standardized test requirement. The appeals court concluded that the standardized test requirement was an "assessment of the outcome" of the students' educational plans.[57] Other courts have determined that requiring disabled students to take standardized tests, including exit exams, does not constitute the denial of a free, appropriate education under IDEA.[58]

Testing low-performing and special-needs students actually helps them by giving them more attention.

The accountability-in-testing movement as reflected in No Child Left Behind and high-stakes tests forces educators to try to lift up every student. In the past, low-performing students were marginalized. Under the new system of accountability, school officials must pay attention to every child's scores. One expert wrote that this system has led to a "very positive diffusion of awareness" in which teachers pay more attention to low-performing and special-needs children. "Increasingly, at the classroom level, educators are becoming more sensitive to the needs and barriers special needs students face when they take tests," wrote Professor Gregory Cizek. "If not driven within the context of once-per-year, high-stakes tests, it is doubtful that such programs would have been witnessed in the daily experiences of many special needs learners."[59]

The same principle applies to the exit exams that many states require for students to obtain their diplomas. A spokesperson for Jack O'Connell, the California superintendent of schools, said in regard to the positive impact of California's exit exam, "Superintendent O'Connell believes that the exam has been a huge benefit for students who do not pass because it forces schools to pay extra attention to those students and help them. Students struggling with the exam get extra skills, more focused instruction and other such resources to help them learn the skills they need for life after high school."[60]

Requiring high school exit exams ensures that students are properly educated and prepared for the world.

As mentioned previously, most recent standardized testing requirements have survived court challenges. More than 20 states require high school exit exams before students can receive their diploma. Courts in California currently are considering challenges to California's high school exit examination, which is known as CAHSEE (California High School Exit Examination). In May 2006, a trial court ruled that the state could not enforce CAHSEE; however, in August 2006,

California State Superintendent of Public Instruction Jack O'Connell

Today's ruling is yet another affirmation that the California High School Exit Exam is here to stay. The California High School Exit Exam is a critical part of California's school accountability system. By requiring passage of the exit exam as a condition of graduation, we give more meaning to a high school diploma. It raises the bar and ensures that students who graduate have necessary skills in mathematics and English-language arts. I am proud that nearly 91 percent of the high school seniors in the class of 2006 met this challenge of higher expectations. I urge students who have yet to pass to continue with their education so they can master these critical skills, and I continue to ask school districts to help these students find an appropriate educational avenue that will help each of them be successful.

Source: News Release, "Schools Chief Jack O'Connell Applauds Second Court of Appeal Decision to Uphold the California High School Exit Exam," September 29, 2006, http://www.cde.ca.gov/nr/ne/yr06/yr06rel118.asp.

a state appeals court reversed the trial court's action, finding that the trial court's ruling to prohibit school officials from denying diplomas to students who failed the exam went too far. "We have concluded that the trial court erred in granting a statewide preliminary injunction enjoining defendants from enforcing the statute mandating the CAHSEE diploma requirement," the court wrote.[61]

Exit exams are important because they prepare students for the real world. They will face these types of tests in seeking employment, and they should be prepared for them. As the newspaper the *California* editorialized:

> But the real harm comes in graduating students who lack the basic reading and math skills needed to survive in the adult world. We're not doing them [or] their prospective employers any favors by lowering the academic bar. The Supreme Court must move quickly to overturn the lower court's misguided ruling, reinstate the exit exam and make a high school diploma worth something for those who've earned one.[62]

The California Business for Education Excellence (a lobby group that represents the business community in state education policy making) made the point very clearly that students need to pass these tests in order to ensure that they are ready for the workforce:

> While it may seem harsh to prevent students from graduating if they've met all the requirements except for passing the CAHSEE, giving them a false sense that they are ready to enter the workforce or college prepared for those challenges is a much worse punishment. It doesn't help students to award them a high school diploma if they graduate without fully comprehending basic reading and math skills.[63]

Summary

Standardized tests are demonized in some circles of education. The tests are important, however, because they help hold the educational system accountable. How can we determine if schools are doing their job if we do not have some form of national guidance by which we can compare and contrast students from across the country? The answer is that we cannot measure educational efforts without standardizing testing. Testing is not done to harm students; it is done to make sure that the students are receiving a quality education. These tests satisfy constitutional standards and provide an important barometer of school and student progress. In addition, standardized tests help ensure that students are prepared to meet the challenges that they will face in the adult world.

High-stakes Standardized Testing Harms Students and Education

Standardized testing has swelled and mutated, like a creature in one of those old horror movies, to the point that it now threatens to swallow our schools whole.[64]

—Alfie Kohn

Teachers know their students better than any single test can. They know the strengths and weaknesses and capabilities of the children with whom they work daily, week in and week out.[65]

—Dale D. Johnson and Bonnie Johnson

In spring 2003, Bridget Green was invited to deliver the commencement address at her upcoming high school graduation. She was the valedictorian at Alcee Fortier Senior High School in New Orleans, Louisiana. Unfortunately, Green was not able to deliver her valedictory speech or receive her diploma because she had failed the math portion of a mandatory graduation exam that students had to pass to receive their diplomas. Green was praised by her teachers as an outstanding student, but she was deprived of receiving her diploma with her classmates because of this standardized test.[66]

With the passage of No Child Left Behind, the United States has increased its obsession with imposing standardized testing on children whether they need it or not. Not only does our country test students at an increasing rate, but also, as the previous chapter indicated, the tests have become increasingly important and impose higher stakes on teachers, school board officials, parents, and students. That is why this is called "high-stakes" testing.

The National Center for Fair & Open Testing warns that there are several "dangerous consequences" associated with these high-stakes standardized tests: (1) "High-stakes tests are unfair

The National Center for Fair & Open Testing

High-stakes testing punishes students, and often teachers, for things that they cannot control. It drives students and teachers away from learning, and at times from school. It narrows, distorts, weakens and impoverishes the curriculum while fostering forms of instruction that fail to engage students or support high-quality learning. In a high-stakes testing environment, the limit to educational improvement is largely dictated by the tests—but the tests are a poor measure of high-quality curriculum and learning. In particular, the emphasis on testing hurts low-income students and students from minority groups. Testing cannot provide adequate information about school quality or progress. High-stakes testing actively hurts, rather than helps, genuine educational improvement.

Source: "The Dangerous Consequences of High-Stakes Standardized Testing," at http://www.fairtest.org/facts/Dangerous%20Consequences.html.

to many students"; (2) "High-stakes testing leads to increased grade retention and dropping out"; (3) "High-stakes testing produces teaching to the tests"; and (4) "High-stakes testing drives out good teaching."[67]

Similarly, Alfie Kohn, a vigorous critic of standardized testing, pointed out six problems associated with standardized testing. He said that what he terms high-stakes testing (1) causes good teachers and principals to leave the teaching profession, (2) causes educators to "become defensive and competitive," (3) leads to widespread cheating, (4) "may turn teachers against students," (5) "may contribute to overspecialization," and (6) "narrows the conversation about education."[68]

Standardized testing is not an accurate way to assess children.

Standardized tests are not the best way to test children and are not the best method to assess student performance. Standardized tests generally do not measure creativity and deep learning; rather, they often favor rote memorization. Standardized tests generally are high-pressure, multiple-choice exams on which a student must circle one "right answer." These tests do not give students the chance to engage and develop critical thinking skills. As the National Center for Fair & Open Testing stated:

> In a high quality education, students conduct science experiments, solve real-world math problems, write research papers, read novels and stories and analyze them, make oral presentations, evaluate and synthesize information from a variety of fields, and apply their learning to new and ill-defined situations. Standardized tests are poor tools for evaluating these important kinds of learning.[69]

Standardized tests, then, focus on a narrow aspect of learning and, arguably, that focus does not include the most important aspects or types of learning. Standardized testing leads to a fundamental restriction or narrowing of the curriculum. In the words of Kohn, "the test essentially becomes the curriculum."[70] Authors Dale D. Johnson and Bonnie Johnson, who spent a year at a rural school in Louisiana, reported that elementary schools are becoming "testing laboratories" in which students learn how to take tests but suffer a loss of instruction about arts, problem solving, and creativity.[71]

Standardized tests favor wealthier students and may be culturally biased.

There is no question that students with greater resources and economic opportunities perform better as a general rule on standardized tests. Alfie Kohn wrote, "For decades, critics have complained that many standardized tests are unfair because the questions require a set of knowledge and skills more likely to be possessed by children from a privileged background."[72]

The tests arguably violate the due process, equal protection, and federal statutory rights of individual students. The first two claims, due process and equal protection, are constitutional

Due Process, Equal Protection, and Title VI

Due process, referenced in the Fifth and Fourteenth Amendments to the U.S. Constitution, is the constitutional equivalent of fundamental fairness. Due process means that the government cannot deprive an individual of life, liberty, or property interest without first going through a fair procedure. **Equal protection** is the constitutional equivalent of equality. It ensures that the government does not treat people in similar situations differently based on race, sex, or another similar characteristic. The Equal Protection Clause is found in the Fourteenth Amendment to the Constitution. **Title VI** is a federal law that prohibits racial discrimination in programs of federal assistance. All three of these claims—due process, equal protection, and Title VI—have been used to challenge standardized tests.

claims based on the language of the Fourteenth Amendment, which provides in part, "nor shall any State deprive any person of life, liberty or property, without due process of law; nor deny to any person within its jurisdiction the equal protection of the laws." The third claim is based on a federal law rather than on the U.S. Constitution.

Due Process

In the past, courts have sometimes determined that standardized tests violate students' rights. Due process requires that students receive some kind of notice and a hearing before being deprived of an interest in life, liberty, and property, and courts have determined that public school students possess a property interest in their diploma. In a 1975 case that involved the suspension of several students without a proper hearing, the U.S. Supreme Court wrote that students' "legitimate entitlement to a public school education" qualifies as a "property interest which is protected by the due process clause."[73]

In *Debra P. v. Turlington*, the 5th U.S. Circuit Court of Appeals explained that the state of Florida could not require students to pass a standardized test in order to receive a diploma.[74] The appeals court noted that the state imposed the standardized test requirement without giving students the opportunity to learn the material in school. Also according to the court, 13 months' notice was not sufficient. It reasoned that the state had not provided adequate notice of the new policy of denying diplomas based on the standardized test results.

Later courts have made clear that public school officials do not satisfy constitutional due process requirements unless they ensure that students are exposed to the material on which they are tested. "Just as a teacher in a particular class gives the final exam on what he or she has taught, so should the state give its final exam on what has been taught in the classroom."[75] Even later court decisions that have upheld testing requirements recognize that students must be given a meaningful opportunity to learn the material. This becomes a problem when schools are underfunded, subject to teacher shortages, and otherwise provide less-than-sufficient educational opportunities.

Equal Protection

Standardized testing presents equal-protection problems because much evidence shows that certain races of students do not perform as well as others on standardized tests. Equal protection ensures that similarly situated individuals are treated equally, and that the government does not treat one race or gender better or worse than another. Equal protection becomes an issue when students of different races perform differently on standardized tests; evidence of such differences in test scores raise the issue that perhaps these tests are discriminatory. Tests do not recognize that students of different cultures may have different learning styles.[76]

FROM THE BENCH

Debra P. v. Turlington, 644 F.2d 397, 403–404 (5th Cir. 1981)

It is clear that in establishing a system of free public education and in making school attendance mandatory, the state has created an expectation in the students. From the students' point of view, the expectation is that if a student attends school during those required years, and indeed more, and if he takes and passes the required courses, he will receive a diploma. This is a property interest as that term is used constitutionally. Although the state of Florida constitutionally may not be obligated to establish and maintain a school system, it has done so, required attendance and created a mutual expectation that the student who is successful will graduate with a diploma. This expectation can be viewed as a state-created "understanding" that secures certain benefits and that supports claims of entitlement to those benefits.

Source: *Debra P. v. Turlington*, 644 F.2d 397, 403-404 (5th Cir. 1981).

Mothers of students attending the Scarsdale Middle School in Scarsdale, New York, speak with the media in May 2001. These mothers were members of a group called STOP, or State Testing Opposed by Parents, which protested standardized tests and the class time used in preparing for them—one of many criticisms of such testing.

The unfortunate reality is that many African-American and Latino students perform worse than their Caucasian counterparts on standardized tests. In the *Debra P.* case, the federal trial court ruled that the Florida Accountability Act of 1976, which imposed an exit exam requirement, also violated equal protection in part because of the history of the lack of educational opportunities afforded to African-American students. The judge reasoned that the exit requirement had to be enjoined, or stopped, for a period of several years because many of the African-American students had received inferior educational opportunities in the form of segregated schooling in their early years. The trial court judge explained, "Punishing the victims of past discrimination for deficits created by an inferior educational environment neither constitutes a remedy nor creates better educational opportunities."[77]

Title VI

The federal law known as Title VI provides, "No person in the United States shall, on the ground of race, color, or national origin, be excluded from participation in, be denied the benefits of, or be subjected to discrimination under any program or activity receiving Federal financial assistance."[78] Title VI has been interpreted to prohibit tests that intentionally discriminate against minorities. It also has been interpreted to prohibit tests that work a significant disparate, or adverse, impact on minority students.

In the American legal system, the legislative branch of the government passes statutes or laws and the executive branch's administrative agencies pass regulations that expound on or explain the meaning of the statutes. At the federal level, this means that the U.S. Congress passed Title VI and the Department of Justice may pass regulations that explain Title VI.

Justice Department regulations on Title VI provide that the law applies when a federal program works an adverse impact on a particular group of people based on race, color, or national

THE LETTER OF THE LAW

U.S. Department of Justice Guideline on Title VI, 28 C.F.R. 42.101(b)

A recipient, in determining the type of disposition, services, financial aid, benefits, or facilities which will be provided under any such program, or the class of individuals to whom, or the situations in which, such will be provided under any such program, or the class of individuals to be afforded an opportunity to participate in any such program, may not, directly or through contractual or other arrangements, utilize criteria or methods of administration which have the effect of subjecting individuals to discrimination because of their race, color, or national origin, or have the effect of defeating or substantially impairing accomplishment of the objectives of the program as respects individuals of a particular race, color, or national origin.

origin. Specifically, the law prohibits programs that "have the effect of defeating or substantially impairing accomplishment of the objectives of the program as respects individuals of a particular race, color, or national origin."[79]

A disparate impact theory of discrimination means that even a superficially neutral policy—a policy that applies to everyone—can be discriminatory if it has a significant adverse impact on a certain group. In other words, if a test is given to 100 Latino students and 100 Caucasian students and 40 Latino students fail and only 10 Caucasian students fail, the test works an adverse impact on the Latino students. The U.S. Supreme Court recognized the disparate-impact theory of discrimination in the employment context as far back as the 1971 decision in *Griggs v. Duke Power Co.*[80] In that decision, the Court prohibited employment practices of requiring high school diplomas and a certain score on an intelligence test to hold certain jobs. Because of a history of unequal educational opportunities and segregation, African-American employees were adversely affected by these requirements. The Court determined that federal civil rights laws prohibited not only "overt discrimination but also practices that are fair in form, but discriminatory in operation."[81]

The principle of the famous Griggs opinion applies in the context of standardized testing in education. If these tests work an adverse impact on minority students, then at the very least they raise the specter of discrimination.

Standardized tests harm English language learners.

Many people who live in the United States of America come from families for whom English is not the primary language spoken. Many schoolchildren come to this country and must learn English as a second language, yet these children must be given the opportunity to obtain an education. They must not be penalized by a standardized testing regime that discriminates against them because English is not their primary language.

One commentator wrote that "significant anecdotal evidence" exists to show that English-language learners are dropping out at alarmingly high rates in part because of the testing regime. The commentator referred to this as the "push out" phenomenon—that many students who do not speak English as their first language are being pushed out of regular high school.[82]

One standardized test should not determine whether a student obtains a diploma.

There are too many consequences for students who fail a single standardized test. One commentator has called for Congress to intervene and pass legislation to prevent students from being denied a diploma or grade advancement based on one test.[83] She wrote:

> Denying a student a high school diploma or holding a student back in a lower grade level is too severe a consequence for

On the California Exit Exam

Critics of the exit exam do raise a good point that blankly expecting every student in a special education program or for whom English is a second language to pass the exit exam is unrealistic.

Students enter special education programs because they do not learn at the same pace or in the same way as what is considered typical of the population. Individual learning plans are developed for them so educators can better meet specific needs, of which there is quite a range. While a majority of special education students ultimately can pass the exam, there are those who won't be able to. In addition, there are students for whom English is not their primary language and simply cannot be expected to master it at the level the exam requires. Consider the immigrant high school junior who possesses a limited grasp of English though in his own language is extremely knowledgeable.

Source: "Our Voice," *The Desert Sun*, January 13, 2006, p. 10B.

failing a single test. Research illustrates that test scores are not exact. A test is merely an estimate of the student's understanding at one particular time. Thus, states should base high stakes decisions upon grades, attendance, teacher recommendations, reading and writing ability, and overall classroom performance rather than upon one high-stakes test.[84]

Summary

Tests are a way of life in the educational system, but standardized testing has threatened to affect the entire system negatively. Standardized tests do not accurately measure what students learn: they test subjects in a superficial way; they discriminate against some minority and lower-income students; and they harm special needs and English-learning students.

Some states have taken standardized testing to another level. They now require students to pass an exit exam before they can graduate from high school. Even if the students pass all their courses, they can be denied their diplomas. This travesty should not be allowed to occur. Schools should go back to the business of real educating and not become obsessed with standardized tests.

Vouchers and Charter Schools Provide Parents with Needed Choices to Improve Education

Vera McFarland, a pastor at the Milwaukee-based church Believers in Christ, had what she termed a "calling from God" to start a church to help inner-city children in the area. McFarland's vision led to the creation of Believers in Christ Christian Academy in an inner-city neighborhood in 1990. The result has been a windfall for many kids in the Milwaukee area who have attended the academy. Every graduate of the academy's high school program has been accepted into college. This thriving school has been able to help countless kids because of a voucher program that began in Milwaukee in 1990.[85]

Ashlii Cobbs was not a motivated student in her Milwaukee public school. Her lack of effort concerned her mother, Margaret Cobbs, who wanted more from her child's school. After much thought, Margaret enrolled Ashlii in a charter school called St. Marcus Lutheran School, which boasted a rigorous academic program. Almost immediately, Mrs. Cobbs noticed a positive change in Ashlii. "She had never spoken of college," Mrs. Cobbs said. "Once she came here and experienced new things, she spoke so much about college."[86] The stories of Believers in Christ and Ashlii Cobbs show that voucher and charter schools can have a positive influence in the lives of numerous students.

Many public school systems have not performed as well as educators, students, teachers, and parents would like. Students deserve the best educational opportunities possible, and their parents deserve choices. Privatizing education simply offered these better opportunities and gives parents added choices for the schooling of their children. There are several alternatives to traditional public schools—which are to varying degrees more private than public—that give parents greater options. These include vouchers, home schooling, and charter schools. These other educational options empower parents to make the choices that best serve their children's needs.

Vouchers give parents more choices for their children's education.

School vouchers are payments made by the government to parents, who then exercise their choice as to where to educate their children. Voucher programs enable children from lower-income families to send their children to private schools, most of which have tuitions that are too high for those children to attend without aid. Critics have charged that vouchers violate the First Amendment principle of separation of church and state because many children attend private religious schools under the state voucher program. The U.S. Supreme Court, however, ruled in *Zelman v. Simmons-Harris* that a voucher school program in Cleveland, Ohio, did not violate the Establishment Clause of the First Amendment.[87] One commentator hailed the ruling as a "great day for choice."[88]

In reality, vouchers help education by empowering parents and making public schools more accountable. Vouchers provide students, particularly low-income students, the opportunity to

Arguments for School Vouchers

Voucher proponents are motivated by a variety of interests, though they are generally united in their criticism of and displeasure with the state of public education.

Some argue that vouchers are an acceptable, and needed, type of educational reform. Their arguments include:

- Vouchers encourage free-market pressures in education, just as in the business sector. These pressures force public schools to perform more efficiently and effectively in order to compete with private schools.

- Vouchers allow parents the freedom to decide where their children can receive the best education, and enable parents to choose schools where their values and ideals are taught and exemplified.

- With vouchers, parents who are concerned about the safety and quality of public schools have other options for educating their children.

- To restrict religious schools from voucher programs amounts to discrimination against religious points of view and limits the free exercise of religion. This argument is based on the idea that excluding religiously affiliated organizations from government programs that are open to anyone else is discriminatory.

Source: John Ferguson, "Vouchers: An Overview," First Amendment Center Online, http://www.firstamendmentcenter.org//rel_liberty/establishment/topic.aspx?topic=vouchers.

attend schools with smaller classes, more resources, and better infrastructure.

Vouchers continue to pick up steam nationally. In July 2006, Senators Lamar Alexander (R.-Tenn.) and John Ensign (R.-Nev.) and Representatives Howard "Buck" McKeon (R.-Calif.) and Sam Johnson (R.-Tex.) introduced the America's Opportunity Scholarship for Kids Act in the Senate and the House. This act would enable poor children in failing schools to leave those schools and attend private schools. The proposed legislation would allow parents of children in schools that have failed for five straight years to receive $4,000 toward private school tuition or a public school outside their child's existing school district. The parents could also seek up to $3,000 per year for extra tutoring for their children.[89]

"Children may be a fraction of today's society but they are 100% of our future. It's time we empower students—and their parents. I want to give these children a choice and a chance," said Representative Johnson.[90] Senator Alexander offered similar sentiments:

> America's Opportunity Scholarships give meaning to the promise of No Child Left Behind. This is about giving low-income families whose children are stuck in low-performing

U.S. Secretary of Education Margaret Spellings on the America's Opportunity Scholarships for Kids

Year after year, some schools fail to live up to the important standards that ensure our students get the education they deserve. President Bush and I believe that families in communities where schools fall short deserve choices when it comes to their children's education.

Today, we are one step closer to ensuring that parents can make choices that strengthen their children's future and give them a great start in life, regardless of their resources or the communities they live in. The President's America's Opportunity Scholarships program will help low-income students in under-performing schools transfer to the private school of their choice or sign up for intensive tutoring after school or during the summer.

We've already seen the power of choice in Washington, DC, when we launched the first federally funded opportunity scholarship program. With this new legislation, we will spread that success to communities across the country and give parents all over America the ability to make wise choices for their children's education.

Source: Statement from Secretary Spellings on America's Opportunity Scholarships Legislation, July 18, 2006, http://www.ed.gov/news/pressreleases/2006/07/07182006.html.

schools the same opportunities as other families. A recent poll found that 62 percent of public school parents have transferred a child out of one school into a better school or have decided where to live based on the schools in that district. This offers a way out for students whose families don't have the money for tuition or the luxury of moving.

Vouchers improve the educational performance of students, particularly students most in need.

Most evidence shows that voucher students who attend schools other than their former public schools perform better academically. The Institute for Justice, a libertarian, public-interest law firm that defends voucher programs nationwide, asserts that "a significant body of high-quality research shows that school choice programs can help raise both student achievement and parental satisfaction."[91] School choice students in Milwaukee, a city with one of the first voucher programs, have graduated at nearly twice the rate as students in traditional public schools. Students who attended Florida schools on vouchers were performing at a much higher rate as well, until a fateful court decision ruled vouchers unconstitutional. Research showed that a school choice program in Charlotte, North Carolina, resulted in students improving their standardized test scores in both reading and math.[92]

The school choice programs not only help students improve academically but also help students who have been most in need for much of the twentieth and early twenty-first centuries—inner-city African-American students who have been forced to attend poorly performing public schools. Professor Michael Leo Owens explained that school voucher programs "offer the only hope available to many poor students trapped in the nation's worst schools. For a limited number of children, they may make a crucial difference. That possibility is enough for black parents to take a chance."[93]

School vouchers are constitutional and do not present First Amendment problems.

The U.S. Supreme Court upheld the constitutionality of a school voucher plan in Cleveland, Ohio, called the Pilot Project Scholarship Program. The state passed the plan after a history of terrible performance in Cleveland city schools, which a lower federal court had called "a crisis of magnitude." An auditor called the problem "a crisis that is perhaps unprecedented in the history of American education."[94] The program distributed vouchers to parents so that they could pay for private school tuition. Fifty-six private schools participated in the program; 46 of those were religious schools. The program was not designed to indoctrinate students with a particular religious belief, however. Rather, it was designed to provide these students with a good education.

Critics charged that the program violated the Establishment Clause of the First Amendment, which provides for separation of church and state. The critics claimed that there was a church–state problem because government money ended

Howard Fuller

Some argue that choice serves only a portion of the population and that we should expend all our resources on a system that—presumably—serves all. I think we should take a lesson from Harriet Tubman's fight against slavery. She fought everyday to end it, but as she waged that battle, she set out to free as many slaves as possible. I believe we must also work hard to improve the traditional public educational system in this country, but in the meantime, we have a moral responsibility to save as many of our children as we can "by any means necessary."

Source: Howard Fuller, "It's Time to Empower Low-Income Parents," U.S. Newswire, August 7, 2006.

up in the coffers of many private religious schools. The majority of the Supreme Court instead focused on the facts that the program was a matter of private choice and neutral toward religion. Chief Justice William Rehnquist noted that prior cases:

> make clear that where a government aid program is neutral with respect to religion, and provides assistance directly to a broad class of citizens who, in turn, direct government aid to religious schools wholly as a result of their own genuine and independent private choice, the program is not readily subject to challenge under the Establishment Clause.[95]

FROM THE BENCH

Chief Justice William Rehnquist in *Zelman v. Simmons-Harris* (2002)

We believe that the program challenged here is a program of true private choice, consistent with *Mueller, Witters,* and *Zobrest,* and thus constitutional. As was true in those cases, the Ohio program is neutral in all respects toward religion. It is part of a general and multifaceted undertaking by the State of Ohio to provide educational opportunities to the children of a failed school district. It confers educational assistance directly to a broad class of individuals defined without reference to religion, i.e., any parent of a school-age child who resides in the Cleveland City School District. The program permits the participation of all schools within the district, religious or nonreligious. Adjacent public schools also may participate and have a financial incentive to do so. Program benefits are available to participating families on neutral terms, with no reference to religion. The only preference stated anywhere in the program is a preference for low-income families, who receive greater assistance and are given priority for admission at participating schools....

There also is no evidence that the program fails to provide genuine opportunities for Cleveland parents to select secular educational options for their school-age children. Cleveland schoolchildren enjoy a range of educational choices: They may

Rehnquist called the program one of "true private choice" and noted that "any objective observer familiar with the full history and context of the Ohio program would reasonably view it as one aspect of a broader undertaking to assist poor children in failed schools, not as an endorsement of religious schooling in general."[96]

Justice Clarence Thomas spoke forcefully in his concurring opinion, emphasizing that the voucher program would benefit African Americans who lived in poverty. According to Justice Thomas, the opponents of the voucher program ignored the importance of the Fourteenth Amendment's broad vision of equal protection. Thomas explained that "the promise of public school education has failed poor inner-city blacks."[97] He wrote:

remain in public school as before, remain in public school with publicly funded tutoring aid, obtain a scholarship and choose a religious school, obtain a scholarship and choose a nonreligious private school, enroll in a community school, or enroll in a magnet school. That 46 of the 56 private schools now participating in the program are religious schools does not condemn it as a violation of the Establishment Clause. The Establishment Clause question is whether Ohio is coercing parents into sending their children to religious schools, and that question must be answered by evaluating all options Ohio provides Cleveland schoolchildren, only one of which is to obtain a program scholarship and then choose a religious school....

The constitutionality of a neutral educational aid program simply does not turn on whether and why, in a particular area, at a particular time, most private schools are run by religious organizations, or most recipients choose to use the aid at a religious school....

In sum, the Ohio program is entirely neutral with respect to religion. It provides benefits directly to a wide spectrum of individuals, defined only by financial need and residence in a particular school district. It permits such individuals to exercise genuine choice among options public and private, secular and religious. The program is therefore a program of true private choice. In keeping with an unbroken line of decisions rejecting challenges to similar programs, we hold that the program does not offend the Establishment Clause.

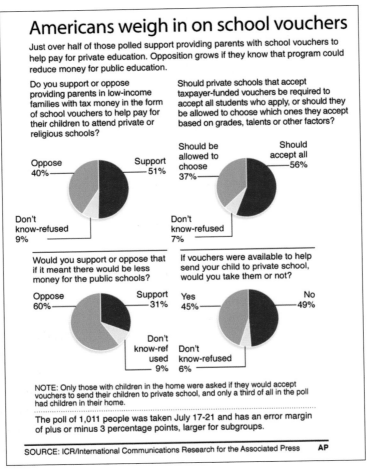

Americans weigh in on school vouchers

Just over half of those polled support providing parents with school vouchers to help pay for private education. Opposition grows if they know that program could reduce money for public education.

Do you support or oppose providing parents in low-income families with tax money in the form of school vouchers to help pay for their children to attend private or religious schools?

Oppose 40%
Support 51%
Don't know-refused 9%

Should private schools that accept taxpayer-funded vouchers be required to accept all students who apply, or should they be allowed to choose which ones they accept based on grades, talents or other factors?

Should be allowed to choose 37%
Should accept all 56%
Don't know-refused 7%

Would you support or oppose that if it meant there would be less money for the public schools?

Oppose 60%
Support 31%
Don't know-refused 9%

If vouchers were available to help send your child to private school, would you take them or not?

Yes 45%
No 49%
Don't know-refused 6%

NOTE: Only those with children in the home were asked if they would accept vouchers to send their children to private school, and only a third of all in the poll had children in their home.

The poll of 1,011 people was taken July 17-21 and has an error margin of plus or minus 3 percentage points, larger for subgroups.

SOURCE: ICR/International Communications Research for the Associated Press   AP

In 2002, Americans were polled on their opinions about school vouchers, which allow parents more freedom in choosing where their children go to school. The results of the poll are shown in the chart above.

While in theory providing education to everyone, the quality of public schools varies significantly across districts. Just as blacks supported public education during Reconstruction, many blacks and other minorities now support school choice programs because they provide the greatest educational opportunities for their children in struggling communities. Opponents of the program raise formulistic concerns about the Establishment Clause but ignore the core purposes of the Fourteenth Amendment.[98]

The net effect of the *Zelman* decision is that there is no federal constitutional bar to a school-choice program that has a primary purpose to simply increase parental choice and improve the educational opportunities for children. Decisions adverse to vouchers have been decided based on state law, not federal law. The better-reasoned state court decisions, such as those made by courts in Wisconsin and Arizona, have recognized the benefit of school-choice programs to their students.

Charter Schools

Charter schools are publicly funded schools that operate under a charter negotiated between the school's organizers and state or local government officials. Charter schools manage the schools without the burden of complying with all the rules and regulations that apply to traditional public schools. Some charter schools are managed by private educational management groups called "education management companies," or EMCs. Charter schools began in Minnesota in 1991, when that state passed the first law establishing a charter school. The next year, a charter school opened in the state. Currently, there are approximately 4,000 charter schools in the country.[99]

The Center for Education Reform (CER) reported in September 2006 that more than 1.15 million students attend nearly 4,000 charter schools nationwide in 40 states.[100] "More and more parents choose to send their children to charter schools, looking for something that works," said CER President Jeanne Allen. "People are recognizing charter schools as new public schools of choice that are accountable for achieving results. It's time to acknowledge that charter schools are no longer an experiment, as the teachers unions like to suggest, but a widely accepted, successful pillar of the public education landscape."[101]

Like vouchers, charter schools have greater flexibility in curricular choices for children. Charter schools can establish

National Catholic Educational Association

The National Catholic Educational Association supports the creation of charter schools as one among several means of expanding opportunities for parental choice in education for all families within the private and public sectors. The Association believes that:

The common good of society is advanced by helping parents to exercise fully their right to direct the upbringing of their children through the educational program of their choice.

Parents must be given a variety of options from which to choose: public, private, religious or charter schools or home schooling.

Charter schools should provide for parental control of educational choice which will exact more accountability from educators while increasing their local autonomy and flexibility.

Charter schools can promote academic excellence by creating a competitive climate, responsive to parental concerns, directed toward improved student performance.

Social justice requires that all parents, especially those of low and limited income whose children are under-served by the public schools, be given meaningful opportunities to create and have their children attend charter schools.

State legislation must expand the market place to allow for a greater number and variety of charter schools with safeguards to ensure that parents are provided with good information to make appropriate comparisons and choices.

Source: NCEA Statement on Charter Schools, http://www.ncea.org/About/NCEAPolicyStatements.asp.

different school hours, different work rules, and school assignment choices that traditional public schools cannot. They also expand educational opportunities for poorer children.

Charter schools are outperforming traditional public schools.

Evidence suggests that charter schools are outperforming traditional public schools because they provide much greater flexibility. For example, test results in the city of Buffalo showed that students at the city's charter schools outperformed the students at traditional public schools on the four major state assessment tests. The charter schools are outperforming the city's public schools even though the charter schools have a greater proportion of students who live below the poverty line.[102] "There are no boundaries to what you can do," Joy Pepper, director of Tapestry Charter School, told the *Buffalo News*. "You can make the program meet the needs of kids with tremendous flexibility. That's huge."[103]

The results are not confined to the city of Buffalo. In Massachusetts, more than 60 percent of charter school students scored better on state assessment tests than their traditional public school peers.[104]

Furthermore, the elevated performance of charter school students has increased the effort of traditional public school administrators to raise the educational levels at their schools. This increased competition helps the students at the traditional public schools as well. Brian P. Golden, a Massachusetts state representative, pointed out, "Kids, not bureaucracies, are our priority, and it's important that we also be attentive to the good that charters have done for students not attending charters."[105]

Summary

Critics claim that choice in education is a bad idea, that increasing the number of voucher and charter schools will drain money from traditional public schools. This criticism ignores the fact that many students in public schools are not receiving a quality education. Poorer children who attend less than fully functioning schools deserve decent educational opportunities. School choice represents, in the words of the Institute for Justice, "the civil rights issue of the 21st century."[106]

In the Legislature: House Resolution in Favor of Charter Schools

RESOLUTION

Congratulating charter schools and their students, parents, teachers, and administrators across the United States for their ongoing contributions to education, and for other purposes.

Whereas charter schools deliver high-quality education and challenge our students to reach their potential;

Whereas charter schools provide thousands of our families with diverse and innovative educational options for their children;

Whereas charter schools are public schools authorized by a designated public entity and are responding to the needs of our communities, families, and students and are promoting the principles of quality, choice, and innovation;

Whereas, in exchange for the flexibility and autonomy given to charter schools, they are held accountable by their sponsors for improving student achievement and for their financial and other operations;

Whereas 41 States, the District of Columbia, and the Commonwealth of Puerto Rico have passed laws authorizing charter schools; ...

Whereas charter schools improve their students' achievement and stimulate improvement in traditional public schools;

Whereas charter schools must meet the student achievement accountability requirements included by the No Child Left Behind Act of 2001, and contained in the Elementary and Secondary Education Act of 1965, in the same manner as traditional public schools, and often set higher and additional individual goals, to ensure that they are of high quality and truly accountable to the public;

Whereas charter schools give parents new freedom to choose their public school, charter schools routinely measure parental satisfaction levels, and charter

In 1954, the U.S. Supreme Court decided one of the major civil-rights issues of the twentieth century when it ruled in *Brown v. Board of Education* that public schools could not be segregated on the basis of race. The Court ruled that such a dual system created feelings of inferiority in African-American children who were given second-class educations. In the twenty-first century,

schools must prove their ongoing success to parents, policymakers, and their communities;

Whereas nearly 40 percent of charter schools report having a waiting list, and the total number of students on all such waiting lists is enough to fill over 1,000 average-sized charter schools;

Whereas charter schools nationwide serve a higher percentage of low-income and minority students than the traditional public school system;

Whereas charter schools have enjoyed broad bipartisan support from the Administration, the Congress, State Governors and legislatures, educators, and parents across the United States; and

Whereas the sixth annual National Charter schools Week, to be held May 1 to 7, 2005, is an event sponsored by charter schools and grassroots charter school organizations across the United States to recognize the significant impacts, achievements, and innovations of charter schools: Now, therefore, be it

Resolved, That—

(1) the House of Representatives acknowledges and commends charter schools and their students, parents, teachers, and administrators across the United States for their ongoing contributions to education and improving and strengthening the public school system of the United States;

(2) the House of Representatives supports the sixth annual National Charter schools Week; and

(3) it is the sense of the House of Representatives that the President should issue a proclamation calling on the people of the United States to conduct appropriate programs, ceremonies, and activities to demonstrate support for charter schools during this week-long celebration in communities throughout the United States.

Source: H.R. 218 (introduced April 2005).

many minority parents in poorer communities still must deal with the harsh reality that nearby public schools are not serving the educational needs of their children. For that reason, school choice presents a great opportunity, a chance for these students to receive a better education. School-choice programs, whether voucher programs that send children to a private school or charter school programs that provide more focused curricula, can help all children, particularly poorer children, achieve better results on tests and a better education. For that reason alone, school-choice programs must be supported.

Privatizing Education and Turning to School Vouchers Are Not the Answer

The voucher is potentially the most devastating weapon in the armory of those warring against the public schools.[107]

—Gerald Bracey

In fall 2006, the Washington, D.C., Public Charter School Board released study results that showed that 118 of the area's 146 charter schools failed to meet academic standards. Many of the students at these charter schools failed portions of the D.C. Comprehensive Assessment. Journalists Theola Labbe and V. Dion Haynes wrote, "The latest test results provide a fuller picture of the paucity of high-achieving schools in the District, despite the expansion of charter schools in the past 10 years as an alternative to the low-performing traditional system."[108] This discouraging development shows that charter schools are not the panacea they are made out to be; rather, it shows that these schools are not superior to public schools.

The school-choice and charter school movements may sound good in theory, but rhetoric must give way to reality. The harsh reality is that vouchers and charter schools divert key monies and resources away from public schools. Some public schools do need to improve, but the answer is not to take needed resources from them. The answer is to increase funding for these schools. If public schools are not performing adequately, then they should be improved. The answer is not to give up on public schools and send away students. The answer is to address the problems at those schools.

There are numerous arguments against vouchers. They take money away from public schools, they divide students based on

Arguments Against Vouchers

- Vouchers will harm public schools by taking the best students, with the most involved parents, out of public schools. This exodus will leave only the most difficult-to-educate children, including special-education students and students with discipline problems. Opponents note that because private schools are not required to take all students, as public schools are, only top students have any real choice. Thus public schools are left with the most-expensive-to-educate children —whom they must now educate with fewer resources.

- Pulling money from public schools will retard "real" school reform, such as smaller class sizes and better resources. Opponents argue that most American youths attend public schools, and school reform should therefore focus on making the public schools better.

- The community will become "Balkanized," as students and families segregate themselves into homogeneous enclaves. A divided and race or religion, they violate the separation of church and state principles found in federal and state constitutions, they do not lead to better education results, they help private schools that are not accountable, and they represent bad public policy. Vouchers take attention and resources away from public schools that do need such increased funding and support.

Vouchers drain money from public schools and lack accountability.

Vouchers drain money from the coffers of public schools. Supporters hail vouchers as increasing choice, but, in reality, they take money away from the public schools that often face increasing

---

suspicious society will result, as students will not have the opportunity to interact with others who are different in a safe and educational environment.

- Providing funding to religious schools violates the principles of the First Amendment's establishment clause as set out in historical documents of the Founding Fathers and Supreme Court jurisprudence, such as *Everson v. Board of Education* (1947).

- While most voucher proposals are based on claims that vouchers allow students trapped in underperforming schools a choice at a better education, the reality is that vouchers don't cover full tuition at most private schools.

- Studies reportedly demonstrate that private school students perform no better than their public school counterparts.

Source: John Ferguson, "Vouchers: Overview," First Amendment Center Online, http://www.firstamendmentcenter.org//rel_liberty/establishment/topic.aspx?topic=vouchers&SearchString=vouchers.

budget deficits. The National Education Association (NEA) argues that there are educational, social, and legal reasons for not supporting vouchers. The association contends that vouchers do not improve student performance, they encourage social and racial stratification, and they subsidize religious practices. "Vouchers rob public school students of scarce resources," said Reg Weaver, president of the NEA. "The buzzword in education today is accountability, yet school vouchers divert scarce public school dollars to unaccountable private schools."[109]

Vouchers not only contribute to a lack of accountability in poorly performing schools, they also drain needed resources away from public schools. Barbara Miner wrote, "While the lack of academic accountability is appalling, the diversion of much-needed dollars away from public education is intolerable."[110]

FROM THE BENCH

Maine Supreme Court in
Anderson v. Town of Durham

The record in this case is sparse as to the nature of the courses taught at the religious schools and their religious practices. Because the religious schools are not participating in this case, those issues are not central to our decision-making. However, it is possible to envision that there may be conflicts between state curriculum, record keeping and anti-discrimination requirements and religious teachings and religious practices in some schools. These conflicts could result in significant entanglement of State education officials in religious matters if religious schools were to begin to receive public tuition funds and the State moves to enforce its various compliance requirements on the religious schools. This concern to avoid excessive entanglements provides a rational basis to maintain the funding limitation in section 2951(2). Parental choice of the school does not sever the religion-state connection when payment is made by a public entity to the religious school and that payment subjects a school's educational and religious practices to state regulation.

Voucher systems violate state constitutions and the separation of church and state.

A bare majority of the U.S. Supreme Court upheld a voucher system in Cleveland, Ohio, in the 2002 case *Zelman v. Simmons-Harris*, but state supreme courts invalidated vouchers in Florida and Maine in 2006. The Maine Supreme Court ruled in *Anderson v. Town of Durham* that the state could prohibit a voucher system that enabled students to attend religious schools. According to the court, such an arrangement created an "excessive entanglement" between church and state.[111]

The Florida Supreme Court invalidated the nation's first statewide voucher program in *Bush v. Holmes*.[112] The Florida court reasoned that the system violated the state constitutional requirement of a uniform system of free public schools. The court wrote that the program "diverts public dollars into separate private systems parallel to and in competition with the free public schools," which are the sole means set out in the state constitution for educating Florida children.[113] The court also expressed concern that the private schools in the program were exempt from many standards imposed by law on public schools, such as mandatory testing.

The four dissenting Supreme Court justices in *Zelman* accurately pointed out that the majority (deciding) opinion distorted existing Establishment Clause doctrine to uphold the voucher program in Cleveland. Justice David Souter noted that the net effect of the ruling will be that public money will pay for religious teachings. He pointed out that 96.6 percent of all voucher recipients go to religious schools. In other words, the state is funding religious schools. Souter bluntly pointed out that "the scale of the aid to religious schools approved today is unprecedented, both in the number of dollars and in the proportion of systemic school expenditure supported."[114] Justice Stephen Breyer expressed another equally powerful concern when he said that the voucher scheme creates a danger of "religiously based social conflict."[115]

FROM THE BENCH

Florida Supreme Court in *Bush v. Holmes*

Although parents certainly have the right to choose how to educate their children, [Florida law] does not . . . establish a "floor" of what the state can do to provide for the education of Florida's children. The provision mandates that the state's obligation is to provide for the education of Florida's children, specifies that the manner of fulfilling this obligation is by providing a uniform, high quality system of free public education, and does not authorize additional equivalent alternatives. . . .

The Constitution prohibits the state from using public monies to fund a private alternative to the public school system, which is what the OSP does. Specifically, the OSP transfers tax money earmarked for public education to private schools that provide the same service—basic primary education. Thus, contrary to the defendants' arguments, the OSP does not supplement the public education system. Instead, the OSP diverts funds that would otherwise be provided to the system of free public schools that is the exclusive means set out in the Constitution for the Legislature to make adequate provision for the education of children. . . .

Even if the tuition paid to the private school is less than the amount transferred from the school district's funds and therefore does not result in a dollar-for-dollar reduction, as the dissent asserts, it is of no significance to the constitutionality of public funding of private schools as a means to making adequate provision for the education of children.

Although opportunity scholarships are not now widely in use, if the dissent is correct as to their constitutionality, the potential scale of programs of this nature is unlimited. Under the dissent's view of the Legislature's authority in this area, the state could fund a private school system of indefinite size and scope as long as the state also continued to fund the public schools at a level that kept them "uniform, efficient, safe, secure, and high quality." However, because voucher payments reduce funding for the public education system, the OSP by its very nature undermines the system of "high quality" free public schools that are the sole authorized means of fulfilling the constitutional mandate to provide for the education of all children residing in Florida. The systematic diversion of public funds to private schools on either a small or large scale is incompatible with [the Florida Constitution].

Charter schools also harm public schools.

Although charter schools are public schools, they are a special type of public school. Too often, these schools create more problems than they solve. Charter schools receive a contract in exchange for greater freedom; however, often, these schools do not fulfill the terms of the contract and there is little oversight of their activities. Many charter schools have had to be shut down for failure to perform. In October 2005, Indianapolis officials voted to close down the Flanner House Higher Learning Center because of widespread problems.[116]

FROM THE BENCH

Justice Stephen Breyer, dissenting in *Zelman v. Simmons-Harris*

The principle underlying these cases—avoiding religiously based social conflict—remains of great concern. As religiously diverse as America had become when the Court decided its major 20th-century Establishment Clause cases, we are exponentially more diverse today. America boasts more than 55 different religious groups and subgroups with a significant number of members....

Under these modern-day circumstances, how is the "equal opportunity" principle to work—without risking the "struggle of sect against sect" against which Justice Rutledge warned? School voucher programs finance the religious education of the young. And, if widely adopted, they may well provide billions of dollars that will do so. Why will different religions not become concerned about, and seek to influence, the criteria used to channel this money to religious schools? Why will they not want to examine the implementation of the programs that provide this money—to determine, for example, whether implementation has biased a program toward or against particular sects, or whether recipient religious schools are adequately fulfilling a program's criteria? If so, just how is the State to resolve the resulting controversies without provoking legitimate fears of the kinds of religious favoritism that, in so religiously diverse a Nation, threaten social dissension?

Source: *Zelman v. Simmons-Harris,* 536 U.S. 639, 723-724 (2002)

Furthermore, studies indicate that charter schools may not be fulfilling their stated goals of improving student achievement. A 2003 study by the National Assessment for Educational Progress found "no measurable difference in performance between charter school students in the fourth grade and their public school counterparts as a whole."[117] A study by the U.S. Department of Education determined that "in five case study states, charter schools are less likely to meet state performance standards than traditional public schools."[118] A 2005 report by Gerald Bracey concluded that charter schools "have not lived up to their promise of increased achievement."[119]

Privatizing public schools in general has not worked.

The push for voucher schools and charter schools is part of a movement among certain circles to call for the privatization of public schools. This movement is not a positive one for public education. Authors Clive R. Belfield and Henry M. Levin wrote in their book *Privatizing Educational Choices* that "there are a number of reasons to be skeptical of the claim that a standardized business model run by a for-profit firm will outperform the public school provision."[120]

The private companies that manage schools often claim that their role increases the improvement of the students. This claim is not always accurate. A report from the American Federation of Teachers (AFT) showed that the academic performance of students at many schools managed by Edison Schools, Inc., lags behind students in comparable public schools. According to the AFT study, 14 out of 20 Edison schools had students performing at a lower level. "This reminds me of when the Raelians recently claimed to have cloned a baby and said they would produce evidence—eventually," said Nancy Van Meier, director of the AFT's Center on Privatization. "Well, there's been no delivery of evidence and no evidence of delivery."[121] These findings have been duplicated in other evaluations of privately managed school systems. The danger of privatizing education is that corporate profits rather than quality education will become the chief goal. The for-profit model could value the bottom line over what works best for the children. Corporate profit could trump teacher quality, better curricula, and the needs of the students.

Summary

Vouchers, charter schools, and the push for privatization all sound good. The call for school choice, parental empowerment, and educational options sounds great. The reality, however, is that all of these plans drain resources from public schools. The public education system is the most important resource in the country, and studies have shown that these new educational choices have not reached their stated goals. The students have not shown great improvement. Instead of focusing on unattainable elixirs or magical cures, we should focus on improving public schools. Some of those who favor vouchers and privatization want to destroy public schools. Author Gerald Bracey referred to it as "the War against America's public schools." He wrote, "A war is being waged on America's public schools. They are under siege. Many entrepreneurs and some former U.S. Department of Education officials are out to destroy them."[122]

Granted, not all of those who favor vouchers and privatization want to destroy public schools. The reality, however, is that these ill-founded movements are harming public schools and not creating the great benefits that they claim. Society should focus on improving traditional public schools rather than just finding fault with them and seeking to replace them.

Continuing Controversy

Three of the leading controversies over educational standards concern the No Child Left Behind Act, standardized testing in general, and school-choice and privatization of public schools. These issues continue to dominate front-page headline news. Readers should keep in mind that many of the subjects mentioned in this book change on a weekly basis. For example, NCLB is up for reauthorization in 2007.

Amending No Child Left Behind

Congress is considering several measures that would amend the No Child Left Behind Act. Some of the measures include the following:

- H.R. 363, called the Keep Our PACT Act, would require full funding for NCLB, particularly "man-

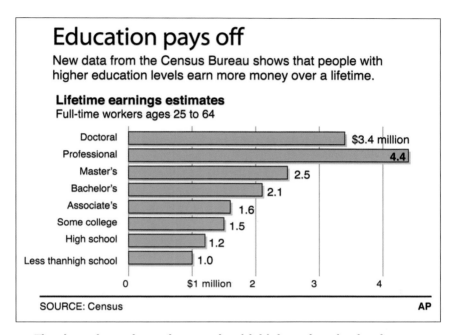

Education pays off
New data from the Census Bureau shows that people with higher education levels earn more money over a lifetime.

Lifetime earnings estimates
Full-time workers ages 25 to 64

Education level	Lifetime earnings
Doctoral	$3.4 million
Professional	4.4
Master's	2.5
Bachelor's	2.1
Associate's	1.6
Some college	1.5
High school	1.2
Less than high school	1.0

SOURCE: Census

AP

The chart above shows that people with higher education levels earn more money over a lifetime. This is just one reason that education will remain a controversial issue in American society; such data makes it clear that education is vital to a person's financial success in life.

datory funding of the Individuals with Disabilities Education Act."

- H.R. 4578 would require "full funding" for No Child Left Behind and would ensure that "states and school districts have the necessary flexibility in implementing" NCLB. The bill would also give school districts an extra four years in order to achieve full proficiency and adequate yearly progress.

- H.R. 4852, the Emergency Moratorium Testing Act of 2006, would impose a three-year moratorium on high-stakes standardized testing. The proposed measure notes that "elected officials at all levels have become obsessed with test results. There is a rush to measure the output of the education community while minimizing the resources contributed by Federal, State, and municipal governments."

- S. 1690, the No Child Left Behind Flexibility and Improvements Act, would give school districts and states greater flexibility in determining what constitutes "adequate yearly progress."

All of these measures were introduced in the 109th Congress, showing that No Child Left Behind is a hotly contested political issue that concerns our legislative leaders. NCLB is up for reauthorization in 2007, and the debate will only intensify. Several lawsuits in different states are challenging various aspects of NCLB.

Similarly, controversies over standardized testing in general continue to dominate the headlines. Litigation over the constitutionality of California's exit exam policy continues. It is possible that an additional court decision could come down before the publication of this book. Interested students and readers should take note that the case is ongoing. Litigation over vouchers in the states of Maine and Arizona also continues. It is very possible that, by the time of this book's publication, another lawsuit concerning school choice could be filed.

Other Educational Standards Issues

There are many other hot-button issues in the field of educational standards in addition to No Child Left Behind, standardized testing, and school vouchers. One of the more prominent concerns the phenomenon of home schooling, which represents the ultimate in privatized education. The U.S. Census Bureau reported that home schooling has increased at a rate of 7 percent to 15 percent each year. Home-schooling parents desire independence from government oversight,[123] and supporters argue that home schooling offers parents the advantage of creating a curriculum that best suits the learning style of their children. The increased flexibility gives students the chance to relax and focus on learning, rather than worry about the regimentation of a traditional public school day.[124]

C.J. Whelan, a teenager who is home schooled, wrote that the pros of home schooling far outweigh any negatives. According to Whelan, a major advantage is that home schooled children have the chance for individualized education.[125]

Opponents counter that home schooling leaves children without the necessary social skills to adapt in the real world. "There's nothing like having the right person with the right experience, skills and tools to accomplish a specific task," wrote Illinois educator Dave Arnold. "Whether it is window-washing, bricklaying or designing a space station. Certain jobs are best left to the pros. Formal education is one of those jobs."[126] Arnold wrote that home-schooled kids do not have the opportunity to develop crucial social skills: "Children should have the opportunity to interact with others their own age. Without allowing

Ruth Snoke, home-schooled teenager

Home-schooling teaches you to adapt to learning at your level, and forces you to create good study habits. You can learn at your own speed, and form your own opinions. A lot of parents home-school because they don't want their children force-fed public-school ideas. As I grow, I am learning to form my own opinions—not those of my parents, per se, but founded on the principles they taught me.

Will I home-school my own kids? If my circumstances are right, it's a good possibility. But the foundation of independence and strength of family that home schooling builds will continue to impact my life forever.

Source: Ruth Snoke, "Home-schooling Has Many Benefits," *Pittsburgh Tribune Review*, May 16, 2006.

their children to mingle, trade ideas and thoughts with others, these parents are creating social misfits."[127]

Another pressing issue that affects educational standards concerns the evolution–creationism debate. Many school boards across the country, from Kansas to Pennsylvania, continue to deal with controversies over the evolution–creationism debate in science classes. Many people believe that science classes should teach evolution—the scientific theory that man descended from lower species—without also having to teach the religious explanation called "creationism." Others argue that teachers should

In the Legislature: Home School Non-Discrimination Act of 2005

Congress finds as follows:

(1) The right of parents to direct the education of their children is an established principle and precedent under the United States Constitution.

(2) Congress, the President, and the Supreme Court, in exercising their legislative, executive, and judicial functions, respectively, have repeatedly affirmed the rights of parents.

(3) Education by parents at home has proven to be an effective means for young people to achieve success on standardized tests and to learn valuable socialization skills.

(4) Young people who have been educated at home are proving themselves to be competent citizens in postsecondary education and the workplace.

(5) The rise of private home education has contributed positively to the education of young people in the United States.

(6) Several laws, written before and during the rise of private home education, are in need of clarification as to their treatment of students who are privately educated at home pursuant to State law.

(7) The United States Constitution does not allow Federal control of home-schooling.

Source: Senate Bill 1692, introduced by Senator Larry Craig, September 13, 2005.

at the least "teach the controversy." President George W. Bush entered the debate in 2005, when he said, "Both sides ought to be properly taught so people can understand what the debate is about. . . . I think that part of education is to expose people to different schools of thought."[128]

The debates are cropping up all over the country. In Pennsylvania, a federal district court invalidated a program that called for the teaching of intelligent design in Dover, Pennsylvania, public schools.[129] (Intelligent design is a belief system that the universe was created by a Creator or Intelligent Designer. It is often viewed as a softer form of creationism.) In Kansas, the state school board changed its science standards several times, vacillating between pro-evolution and anti-evolution positions.[130] Other public school districts struggle with whether to adopt courses on the Bible.[131]

Still other debates occur with respect to teacher certification standards and teacher pay. Legislation at the federal level attempts to address the problems of teacher shortages in this crucial era of education. Representative George Miller, one of the key craftsmen of part of the No Child Left Behind Act, recently introduced the Teachers Excellence for All Children Act of 2005.[132] This legislation seeks to increase the number of teachers, particular minority teachers, in the classrooms.

Funding for Education

Another major issue in the educational standards arena concerns education funding. This has been a controversial issue for a long time. Many people believe that schools should be funded on a more equal basis. Others believe that the problem is not in the specific allocation of monies to each school but in how the available money is spent. Some people believe that more education funding should go directly to classrooms. First Class Education, an organization devoted to school reform, advocates that at least 65 percent of all education funding should go directly to expenses in classrooms. This is called the "65 percent solution."

In the Legislature: Teacher Excellence for All Children Act of 2005

The Congress finds as follows:

(1) There are not enough qualified teachers in the Nation's classrooms, and an unprecedented number of teachers will retire over the next 5 years. Over the next decade, the Nation will need to bring 2,000,000 new teachers into public schools.

(2) Too many teachers and principals do not receive adequate preparation for their jobs.

(3) More than one-third of children in grades 7–12 are taught by a teacher who lacks both a college major and certification in the subject being taught. Rates of "out-of-field teaching" are especially high in high-poverty schools.

(4) Seventy percent of math classes in high-poverty middle schools are assigned to teachers without even a minor in math or a related field.

(5) Teacher turnover is a serious problem, particularly in urban and rural areas. Over one-third of new teachers leave the profession within their first 3 years of teaching, and 14 percent of new teachers leave the field within the first year. After 5 years—the average time it takes for teachers to maximize students' learning—half of all new teachers will have exited the profession. Rates of teacher attrition are highest in high-poverty schools. Between 2000 and 2001, 1 out of 5 teachers in the Nation's high-poverty schools either left to teach in another school or dropped out of teaching altogether.

(6) Fourth graders who are poor score dramatically lower on the National Assessment of Educational Progress (NAEP) than their counterparts. Over 85 percent of fourth graders who are poor failed to attain NAEP proficiency standards in 2003.

(7) African-American, Latino, and low-income students are much less likely than other students to have highly-qualified teachers.

(8) Research shows that individual teachers have a great impact on how well their students learn. The most effective teachers have been shown to be able to boost their pupils' learning by a full grade level relative to students taught by less effective teachers.

(9) Although nearly half (42 percent) of all teachers hold a master's degree, fewer than 1 in 4 secondary teachers have a master's degree in the subject they teach.

(10) Young people with high SAT and ACT scores are much less likely to choose teaching as a career. Those who have higher SAT or ACT scores are twice as likely to leave the profession after only a few years.

(11) Only 16 States finance new teacher induction programs, and fewer still require inductees to be matched with mentors who teach the same subject.

Source: H.R. 2835: Teacher Excellence for All Children Act of 2005, http://www.govtrack. us/congress/bill.xpd?bill=h109-2835.

"The public debate over school spending is typically over more or less," said Patrick Byrne, head of First Class Education. "The real debate should be: What are we spending it on?"[133]

Summary

There are no easy answers to many of the controversies with respect to educational standards. No Child Left Behind,

Dr. Patrick Byrne

Ben Franklin famously said, "A penny saved is a penny earned." For K–12 education funding, a few pennies saved could mean literally billions of dollars earned for America's classrooms. That's the driving force behind First Class Education, a thriving national movement to enact the 65% Solution.

It's a simple idea. If we can get the business side of education to adopt better business practices, we would have more money for the education side of education. Business schools throughout America teach management techniques called "best practices" and "benchmarking"—determine what the most efficient companies in a given field are doing and apply similar goals for your firm. In the business of K–12 public school education, First Class Education proposes the benchmark of placing 65% of operational budgets in the classroom.

According to the National Center for Education Statistics (NCES), just four years ago seven states across America—from Utah to Maine, Tennessee to New York—placed at least 65% of their operational budgets in the classroom. Now only two states do. Four years ago fourteen states placed less than 60% of their budgets in the classroom. Now twenty states aren't even getting 60% to their classrooms. The NCES has reported dramatic recent increases in K–12 education funding—four times the rate of inflation—while for four straight years the percentage of dollars reaching America's classrooms has declined. Just 61.3% is now reaching our classrooms as a national average. We can and must do better.

Source: Patrick M. Byrne, *Chairman's Corner*, http://www.firstclasseducation.org/chariman-remarks.asp.

high-stakes standardized testing, vouchers, charter schools, home schooling, teacher certification, the evolution–creationism debate, and educational funding are all divisive issues. The important factor is that we continue to strive for public debate, dialogue, and discussion of these important matters. Nearly everyone agrees with Chief Justice Earl Warren's statement in the *Brown v. Board of Education* decision about the importance of education. His statement remains as true today as it was on May 17, 1954: "Education is perhaps the most important function of state and local governments."

Introduction: Educational Standards

1. *Brown v. Board of Education,* 347 U.S. 483, 493 (1954).

2. "President Signs Landmark No Child Left Behind Education Bill," January 8, 2002, http://www.whitehouse.gov/news/releases/2002/01/20020108-1.html.

3. Statement of Secretary Spellings on Fourth Anniversary of No Child Left Behind, January 9, 2006, http://www.ed.gov/news/pressreleases/2006/01/01092006.html.

4. Gerald W. Bracey, *What You Should Know About the War Against America's Public Schools.* Boston: Allyn and Bacon, 2003, p. 70.

5. Peter Sacks, *Standardized Minds: The High Price of America's Testing Culture and What We Can Do to Change It.* Cambridge, Mass.: Perseus Books, 1999.

6. S.B. 3682 (2006) and H.R. 5822 (2006).

Point: No Child Left Behind Is a Positive Force for Improving Our Nation's Public Schools

7. Statement of President Bush at signing of No Child Left Behind Act, January 8, 2002, http://www.whitehouse.gov/news/releases/2002/01/20020108-1.html.

8. Ibid.

9. Frederick M. Hess and Michael J. Petrilli, *No Child Left Behind Primer.* New York: Peter Lang, 2006, pp. 63–65.

10. Statement of Rebecca Pringle on behalf of the National Education Association before the Aspen Institute's Commission on No Child Left Behind, August 4, 1006, http://www.nea.org/lac/esea/080406testi.html.

11. National Commission on Excellence in Education, *A Nation at Risk: The Imperative for Educational Reform* (April 1983), http://www.ed.gov/pubs/NatAtRisk/index.html.

12. "Recommendations" section of *A Nation at Risk,* http://www.ed.gov/pubs/NatAtRisk/recomm.html.

13. Carl Campanile, "Klein Gives Powerful 'No Child' Defense," *New York Post,* May 10, 2006, p. 2.

14. Ruben Navarrett Jr. "Defending No Child Left Behind," *The San Diego Union-Tribune,* March 1, 2006, http://www.signonsandiego.com/union-trib/20060301/news_lz1e1navarr.html.

15. Written testimony of Kati Haycock, director of the Education Trust, to the House Committee on Education and the Workforce, September 29, 2005, http://www2.edtrust.org/EdTrust/Press+Room/Haycock+Testimony+9.29.05.htm.

16. Hess and Petrilli, *No Child Left Behind,* pp. 44–45.

17. Ibid., p. 63.

18. Phyllis McClure, Diane Piche, and William L. Taylor, *Days of Reckoning: Are States and the Federal Government Up to the Challenge of Ensuring a Qualified Teacher for Every Student* [study], Citizens' Commission on Civil Rights (July 2006), p. 1, http://www.cccr.org/DaysofReckoning.pdf.

19. Department of Education, "No Child Left Behind: A Toolkit for Teachers: What Does 'Highly Qualified' Mean for Teachers?," http://www.ed.gov/teachers/nclbguide/toolkit_pg6.html#provision.

20. Speech of Sandra Feldman, President of American Federation of Teachers, at 2001 White Conference on Preparing Tomorrow's Teachers, 2001, http://www.ed.gov/admins/tchrqual/learn/preparingteachersconference/feldman.html.

Counterpoint: No Child Left Behind Is a Misguided Law That Does More Harm Than Good

21. Linda Darling-Hammond, "No Child Left Behind: The Collision of New Standards and Old Inequalities," in *Many Children Left Behind,* ed. Deborah Meier and George Wood. Boston: Beacon Press, 2004, p. 9.

22. Natalia Mielczarek, "NCLB critic a hit with teachers," *The Tennessean,* November 19, 2006, p. B1.

23. Ibid., p. 4.

24. James E. Ryan, "The Perverse Incentives of the No Child Left Behind Act." 79 N.Y.U. L. Rᴇᴠ. 932, 933 (2004).

25. Ibid., p. 934.

26. Darling-Hammond, "No Child Left Behind," p. 16.

27. Testimony of National Council for the Social Studies before House Committee on Education and the Workforce, http://static.ncss.org/files/media/NCSS%20testimony%200518.pdf.

28. Sam Dillon, "Schools Cut Back Subjects to Push Reading and Math," *The New York Times*, March 26, 2006, http://www.nytimes.com/2006/03/26/education/26child.html?ex=1301029200en=0c91b5bd32dabe2aei=5088partner=rssnytemc=rss.

29. Center on Education Policy, "NCLB Policy Brief—NCLB: Narrowing the Curriculum," July 2005, http://www.cep-dc.org/nclb/NCLBPolicyBriefs2005/CEP-PB3web.pdf.

30. Center on Education Policy, "Majority of School Leaders Report Gains in Achievement, but a Narrower Curriculum Focus Under No Child Left Behind," March 2006, http://www.cep-dc.org/nclb/Year4/Press/CEPNewsRelease24March2006.doc.

31. National Council for the Social Studies, "Joint Organizational Statement on No Child Left Behind," (2004), http://www.socialstudies.org/jointNCLBstatement.

32. Thomas Misco, "In Response to NCLB: Retaining the Social Studies," Essays in Education (2005), http://www.usca.edu/essays/vol152005/misco.pdf, p. 8.

33. 411 U.S. 1 (1973).

34. Ibid., p. 54.

35. Statement of Connecticut Attorney General Richard Blumenthal, August 22, 2005, http://www.ct.gov/ag/cwp/view.asp?A=1949&Q=300456.

36. National Education Association, "Questions and Answers about *Pontiac v. Spellings*," (2005) http://www.nea.org/lawsuit/questions.html.

37. Howard Fischer, "Lawsuit Seeks Relief in How Schools Are Assessed," *Arizona Daily Star,* July 6, 2006, http://www.azstarnet.com/sn/printDS/136806.

38. H.R. 363.

39. Representative Chris Van Hollen, "Van Hollen Introduces Bill to 'Keep Our Promise' to American Schoolchildren," January 26, 2005, at http://www.house.gov/vanhollen/press2005/keepourpromisesrelease.html.

40. H.R. 1506 and S. 726 (introduced April 2006).

Point: Standardized Testing Motivates Students and Creates Accountability in Schools

41. Ken Rodriguez, "Learning Curve; Semi-literate Football Star Is Now an Educator," *San Antonio Express News,* June 30, 2002, p. 1C.

42. Stephen G. Sireci, "The Most Frequently Unasked Questions about Testing," in *Defending Standardized Testing*, ed. Richard P. Phelps. Mahwah, NJ: Lawrence Erlbaum Associates, 2005, pp. 111–121, 114–116.

43. Gregory J. Cizek, "High-Stakes Testing: Contexts, Characteristics, Critiques, and Consequences," in *Defending Standardized Testing*, ed. Richard P. Phelps. Mahwah, N.J.: Lawrence Erlbaum Associates, 2005, pp. 23–54.

44. Sireci, "The Most Frequently Unasked Questions," pp. 111–121, 113.

45. Ibid.

46. "LEAP, Why Are We Talking About High-Stakes Testing Now," *The Daily World,* February 6, 2005, p. 9A.

47. Richard P. Phelps, "Forty Years of Public Opinion," in *Defending Standardized Testing*, ed. Richard P. Phelps. Mahwah, NJ: Lawrence Erlbaum Associates, 2005, p. 11.

48. Jocelyn Wiener, "Minority Parents Support Exit Exam," *The Sacramento Bee,* August 24, 2006, at A1.

49. "California at the Crossroads: Embracing the CAHSEE and Moving Forward," August 22, 2006, http://www2.edtrust.org/NR/rdonlyres/034BB0E2-2710-4AE2-829B-6631BFA84462/0/CAattheCrossroads2006.pdf.

50. 644 F.2d 3977 (5th Cir. 1981).

51. 87 F.Supp.2d 667 (W.D. Tex. 2000).

52. Ibid., p. 671.

53. Ibid., p. 675.

54. Ibid., p. 679.

55. Ibid., p. 680.

56. *Rene v. Reed,* 751 N.E.2d 736 (Ind.App. 2001).

57. Ibid., p. 747.

58. Mary Nebgen, "California's High School Exit Examination: Passing the Test," 31 McGeorge L Rev 359, 382-384. (2000); *Board of Education v. Ambach,* 436 N.Y.S2d 564 (1981); *Brookhart v. Illinois State Board of Education,* 697 F.2d 179 (7th Cir. 1983).

59. Cizek, "High-Stakes Testing," p. 37.

60. E. Ashley Wright, *The California Aggie* (via the University Wire), May 15, 2006.

61. *O'Connell v. Superior Court,* 47 Cal. Rptr.3d 147 (Cal.App.4th 2006).

62. "At Many High School Graduation Ceremonies, Students Are Handed a Mock Diploma" [editorial], *The Californian,* May 24, 2006, p. 4B.

63. California Business for Education Excellence, "Judge's Decision to Suspend Exit Exam Is Bad for Students," PR Newswire, May 12, 2006.

Counterpoint: High-stakes Standardized Testing Harms Students and Education

64. Alfie Kohn, *The Case Against Standardized Testing.* Portsmouth, NH: Heinemann, 2000, p. 1).

65. Dale D. Johnson and Bonnie Johnson, *High Stakes: Children, Testing and Failure in American Schools.* Lanham, Md.: Rowman & Littlefield Publishers, 2002, p. 204.

66. Aesha Rasheed, "Falling Short; The Graduate Exit Exam Stopped Bridget Green From Being Valedictorian," *Times-Picayune,* August 10, 2003, p. 1.

67. The National Center for Fair & Open Testing, "The Dangerous Consequences of High-Stakes Standardized Testing," http://www.fairtest.org/facts/Dangerous%20Consequences.html.

68. Ibid., pp. 27–29.

69. The National Center for Fair & Open Testing, "The Limits of Standardized Tests for Diagnosing and Assisting Student Learning," http://www.fairtest.org/facts/Limits%20of%20Tests.html.

70. Ibid., p. 29.

71. Johnson and Johnson, *High Stakes* p. 203.

72. Kohn, *Case Against Standardized Testing,* p. 36.

73. *Goss v. Lopez,* 419 U.S. 565, 584 (1975).

74. 644 F.2d 397 (5th Cir. 1981).

75. Ibid., p. 406.

76. Jean T. Pryce, "A Brief Overview of High-Stakes Testing and Its Implications for Historically Underserved Students," in *The Impact of High-Stakes Testing on the Academic Futures of Non-Mainstream Students,* ed. Gail Singleton Taylor. Lewiston, N.Y.: The Edwin Mellen Press, 2004, p. 1.

77. *Debra P. v. Turlington,* 474 F.Supp. 244, 257 (M.D. Fla. 1979).

78. 42 U.S.C. 2000d.

79. 28 C.F.R. 42.101(b).

80. 401 U.S. 424 (1971).

81. Ibid., p. 431.

82. Janet M. Hostetler, "Testing Human Rights: The Impact of High-Stakes Tests on English-Language Learners Right to Education in New York City." 30 N Y U Rev L & Soc Change 483, 497–498 (2006).

83. Betsy A. Gerber, "High Stakes Testing: A Potentially Discriminatory Practice with Diminishing Legal Relief for Students at Risk." 75 Temple Law Rev 863, 889 (2002).

84. Ibid.

Point: Vouchers and Charter Schools Provide Parents with Needed Choices to Improve Education

85. Sarah Carr, "Mission accomplished: How one Milwaukee school has built

a thriving voucher school that sends its graduates to college," *Milwaukee Journal Sentinel,* June 13, 2005, http://www.jsonline.com/story/index. aspx?id=333272.

86. Sarah Carr, "New School, New Attitude: Ashli Cobbs, Once a Struggling Student, Now Soars," *Milwaukee Journal Sentinel,* June 14, 2005, http://www.jsonline.com/story/index.aspx?id=333498.

87. 536 U.S. 639 (2002).

88. Murdock Gibbs. "A Great Day for Choice," *Chicago Independent Bulletin,* August 1, 2002, http://www.exodusnews. com/editorials/editorial-094.htm.

89. "Senate and House Education Leaders Introduce Legislation to Give Children Trapped in Under-Performing Schools More Opportunities to Achieve," July 18, 2006, http://alexander.senate.gov/index.cfm?FuseAction=PressReleases. Detail&PressRelease_id=1040&Month=7&Year=2006.

90. "House and Senate Education Leaders Introduce Legislation to Give Children Trapped in Under-Performing Schools More Opportunities to Achieve" [press release], July 18, 2006, http://www.sam-johnson.house.gov/News/Document-Print.aspx?DocumentID=47202.

91. Institute for Justice, "School Choice Works: Evidence of Improved Academic Achievement," http://www.ij.org/pdf_folder/school_choice/academic_results. pdf.

92. Ibid.

93. Michael Leo Owens, "Why Blacks Support Vouchers," *The New York Times,* February 26, 2002, p. A25.

94. *Zelman v. Simmons-Harris,* 536 U.S. 639, 644 (2002).

95. Ibid., p. 652.

96. Ibid., p. 655.

97. Ibid., p. 682.

98. Ibid., p. 682 (J. Thomas, concurring).

99. Sandra Vergari, "Charter Schools: A Significant Precedent in Public Education." 59 N.Y.U. Ann Surv Am L 495, 496 (2003).

100. Center for Education Reform, "Charter Schools Number Nearly 4,000 Nationwide," September 29, 2006, http://www. edreform.com/index.cfm?fuseAction= document&documentID=2497&section ID=34&NEWSYEAR=2006.

101. Ibid.

102. Peter Simon, "Charters Outperform Buffalo City Schools," *Buffalo News,* October 30, 2005, p. A1.

103. Ibid.

104. Brian P. Golden, "As You Were Saying: Maintain Charter Schools as Engine of Reform for System," *The Boston Herald,* April 25, 2004, p. 026.

105. Ibid.

106. Clark Neily, "The Florida Supreme Court vs. School Choice: A "Uniformly" Horrid Decision," 10 Tex. Rev. Law & Pol. 401, 402 (2006).

Counterpoint: Privatizing Education and Turning to School Vouchers Are Not the Answer

107. Gerald W. Bracey, *What You Should Know,* p. 137.

108. Theola Labbe and Dion Haynes, "Most Charter Schools Miss Test Benchmarks," *Washington Post,* September 27, 2006, p. B04.

109. National Education Association, "National School Voucher Legislation Announced by Congressional Leaders and Education Secretary," July 18, 2006, http://www.nea.org/newsreleases/2006/nr060718.html.

110. Barbara Miner, "Milwaukee Schools Evidence of Vouchers' False Promise; Public System Underfunded, Private Schools Unaccountable," *Lexington Herald Leader,* April 26, 2003, p. A13.

111. *Anderson v. Town of Durham,* 895 A.2d 944 (Me. 2006), http://www. courts.state.me.us/opinions/ 2006%20documents%2006me39an.htm.

112. 919 So.2d 392 (Fla. 2006).

113. Ibid., p. 398.

114. *Zelman v. Simmons-Harris,* 536 U.S. 639, 708 (2002)(J. Souter, dissenting).

115. Ibid. at 717 (J. Breyer, dissenting).

116. Associated Press, "Indianapolis to Shut Down Troubled Charter High School," October 24, 2005.

117. National Assessment of Educational Progress, America's Charter Schools: "Results from the NAEP 2003 Pilot Study," (2003), http://nces.ed.gov/nationsreportcard/studies/charter/2005456.asp.

118. Department of Education, "Evaluation of the Public Charter Schools Program: Final Report," at Evaluation of the Public Charter Schools Program: Final Report," (2003), http://www.ed.gov/rschstat/eval/choice/pcsp-final/execsum.html.

119. Gerald Bracey, "Charter Schools' Performance and Accountability: A Disconnect" [policy brief], Arizona State University, 2005, http://www.asu.edu/educ/epsl/EPRU/documents/EPSL-0505-113-EPRU.pdf, p. 2.

120. Clive R. Barfield and Henry M. Levin, *Privatizing Educational Choice: Consequences for Parents, Schools, and Public Policy.* Boulder, Colo.: Paradigm Publishers, 2005, p. 171.

121. American Federation of Teachers, "AFT Report on Edison Schools Finds Achievement Worse than Edison Claims," February 18, 2003, http://65/110.81.56/presscenter/releases/2003/0218103.htm.

122. Bracey, *What You Should Know,* p. 3.

Conclusion: Continuing Controversy

123. Michael Smith, "Home-Schooling Today," *The Washington Times,* December 19, 2005, p. B04.

124. Chris Stuccio, "Home Schooling Offers Many Advantages," *Buffalo News,* June 30, 2006, p. A8.

125. C.J. Whelan, "I'm Finding Home-Schooling Meets My Needs," *Sebastian Sun,* May 5, 2006, p. A5.

126. Dave Arnold, "Home Schools Run by Well-Meaning Amateurs," http://www.nea.org/espcolumns/dv040220.html.

127. Ibid.

128. David L. Hudson, Jr., "Evolution and Creationism: Overview" (updated January 2006), First Amendment Center Online, http://www.firstamendmentcenter.org/rel_liberty/publicschools/topic.aspx?topic=evolution_creation.

129. See *Kitzmiller v. Dover Area School Board,* 404 F.Supp. 2d 707 (M.D. Pa. 2005), opinion accessible at http://www.pamd.uscourts.gov/kitzmiller/kitzmiller_342.pdf.

130. Associated Press, "Evolution opponents lose control of Kan. education board," First Amendment Center Online, August 6, 2006, http://www.firstamendmentcenter.org/news.aspx?id=17230.

131. Associated Press, "High schools try out new Bible course," First Amendment Center Online, October 6, 2006, http://www.firstamendmentcenter.org/news.aspx?id=17469.

132. H.R. 2835 (2005).

133. Patrik Jonsson, "How Much Education Funding Should Go Directly to Classrooms?" *Christian Science Monitor,* January 25, 2006, http://www.csmonitor.com/2006/0125/p01s03-legn.html.

Books and Articles

Barfield, Clive R., and Henry M. Levin. *Privatizing Educational Choice: Consequences for Parents, Schools, and Public Policy*. Boulder, Colo.: Paradigm Publishers, 2005.

Berliner, David C., and Bruce J. Biddle. *The Manufactured Crisis: Myths, Frauds and the Attack on America's Public Schools*. Reading, Mass.: Addison-Wesley, 1995.

Bracey, Gerald W. "Charter Schools' Performance and Accountability: A Disconnect," Arizona State University, 2005, http://www.asu.edu/educ/epsl/EPRU/documents/EPSL-0505-113-EPRU.pdf.

Bracey, Gerald W. *What You Should Know About the War Against America's Public Schools*. Boston: Allyn and Bacon, 2003.

DeJarnett, Susan L. "The Philadelphia Story: The Rhetoric of School Reform." 72 UMKC L Rev 949 (2004).

Gaylor, Keith, et al. *State High School Exit Exams: A Maturing Reform*. Center on Education Policy, August 2004, http://www.cep-dc.org/highschoolexit/ExitExamAug2004/ExitExam2004.pdf.

Gerber, Betsy. "High Stakes Testing: A Potentially Discriminatory Practice with Diminishing Legal Relief for Students at Risk." 75 Temple L Rev 863 (2002).

Hess, Frederick M., and Michael J. Petrilli. *No Child Left Behind Primer*. New York: Peter Lang, 2006.

Hostetler, Janet M. "Testing Human Rights: The Impact of High-Stakes Tests on English-Language Learners Right to Education in New York City." 30 N.Y.U. Rev. L. & Soc. Change 483 (2006).

Jencks, C., and M. Phillips, eds. *The Black-White Test Score Gap*. Washington, D.C.: Brookings Institution Press, 1998.

Johnson, Dale D., and Bonnie Johnson. *High Stakes: Children, Testing and Failure in American Schools*. Lanham, Md.: Rowman & Littlefield Publishers, 2002.

Kohn, Alfie. *The Case Against Standardized Testing*. Portsmouth, N.H.: Heinemann, 2000.

Meier, Deborah, and George Wood, eds. *Many Children Left Behind: How the No Child Left Behind Is Damaging Our Children and Our Schools*. Boston: Beacon Press, 2004.

A Nation at Risk: The Imperative for Educational Reform, April 1983, http://www.ed.gov/pubs/NatAtRisk/index.html.

Phelps, Richard P., ed. *Defending Standardized Testing.* Mahwah, N.J.: Lawrence Erlbaum Associates, 2005.

Popham, W.J. *The Truth About Testing: An Educator's Call to Action.* Alexandria, Va.: Association for Supervision and Curriculum, 2001, p. l.

Rothstein, Richard. *The Way We Were? The Myths and Realities of America's Student Achievement.* New York: Century Foundation Press, 1998.

Sacks, Peter. *Standardized Minds: The High Price of America's Testing Culture and What We Can Do to Change It.* Cambridge, Mass.: Perseus Books, 1999.

Solomon, Lewis D. "Edison Schools and the Privatization of K-12 Public Education: A Legal and Policy Analysis." 30 FORDHAM URB LJ 1281 (2003).

Sundermann, G., and J. Kim. *Inspiring Vision, Disappointing Results: Four Studies on Implementing the No Child Left Behind Act.* Cambridge, Mass.: Harvard Civil Rights Project, 2004.

Taylor, Gail Singleton, ed. *The Impact of High-Stakes Testing on the Academic Futures of Non-Minority Students.* Lewiston, N.Y.: The Edwin Mellen Press, 2004.

Vergari, Sandra. "Charter Schools: A Significant Precedent in Public Education." 59 N.Y.U. ANN SURV AM L 495 (2003).

Web Sites
American Federation of Teachers
http://www.aft.org/
This site for teachers has information on a wide variety of education issues, including the 65 percent solution, charter schools, English language learners, No Child Left Behind, privatization, standards-based reform, and vouchers.

Center on Education Policy
http://www.cep-dc.org/
According to its site, this group is "a national, independent advocate for public education and for more effective public schools."

Education Trust-West
http://www2.edtrust.org/edtrust/etw/
This civil rights group favors at least some standardized tests while focusing on increasing the achievement levels of minority students.

First Class Education
http://www.firstclasseducation.org/
This reform-based organization calls for 65 percent of education money to go directly to classroom spending.

Institute for Justice
http://www.ij.org
This self-described libertarian public interest law firm has a section on its Web site devoted to its school choice litigation on behalf of voucher programs.

National Assessment of Educational Progress
http://nces.ed.gov/nationsreportcard/
This organization's site has links to numerous studies regarding standard-based education.

National Center for Fair & Open Testing
http://www.fairtest.org
This group provides much information that is critical of current standardized testing.

No Child Left Behind Act
http://www.nabe.org/documents/policy_legislation/NCLBAct.pdf
This is the actual language of the controversial law.

U.S. Department of Education
http://www.ed.gov/index.jhtml
This government site contains a wealth of relevant information on educational standards issues.

U.S. Department of Justice guidelines on Title VI
http://www.usdoj.gov/crt/cor/coord/titlevi.htm

Cases and Statutes

Anderson v. Town of Durham, 895 A.2d 944 (Me. 2006)

The Maine Supreme Court struck down a school voucher system, finding that it would create an excessive entanglement between church and state. The state's high court reasoned that there could be "significant conflict" between the state's goals and some of the school's religious teachings.

Brown v. Board of Education of Topeka, Kansas, 347 U.S. 483 (1954)

The U.S. Supreme Court unanimously ruled that segregated public schools violate the equal protection clause of the Fourteenth Amendment. The Court reasoned that such segregated schools were "inherently unequal."

Bush v. Holmes, 919 So.2d 392 (Fla. 2006)

The Florida Supreme Court ruled that a state voucher program was unconstitutional because it violated the state constitutional requirement of a uniform system of free public education. The court expressed concern that the private schools in the voucher program would be exempt from state standards imposed on public schools.

Connecticut v. Spellings, No. 305CV1330 (U.S. Dist. Ct.)(8/22/2005)

This federal lawsuit alleges that the NCLB unconstitutionally forces the state of Connecticut to spend too much of its own money to meet federal demands. This lawsuit is still ongoing.

Debra P. v. Turlington, 644 F.2d 397 (5th Cir. 1981)

A federal appeals court ruled that the state of Florida could not require students to pass a standardized test in order to receive their diploma. The court decided the case on due-process grounds—that the students did not receive adequate notice of the test and its heavy consequences.

GI Forum Image De Tejas v. Texas Educ. Agency, 87 F.Supp. 2d 667 (W.D. Tex. 2000)

A federal district court rejected constitutional challenges to a standardized test in Texas schools. The court viewed the test not as an agent of discrimination, but a valid, objective way to measure accountability in schools.

Griggs v. Duke Power Co., 401 U.S. 424 (1971)

The U.S. Supreme Court ruled that an employer could not rely on standardized tests that were not related to job performance. The Court recognized that the tests worked a disparate, or adverse, impact on African-American workers.

Pontiac v. Spellings, No. 05-CV-71535-DT (E.D. MI)

This ongoing lawsuit alleges that Congress failed to fulfill its funding promises under NCLB.

San Antonio Independent School District v. Rodriguez, 411 U.S. 1 (1973)

The U.S. Supreme Court ruled that the state of Texas could fund schools with local property taxes. The Court's decision meant that poorer schools would not have the resources of richer schools.

Zelman v. Simmons-Harris, 536 U.S. 639 (2002)

The U.S. Supreme Court upheld a voucher program for Cleveland schools, finding that it was a program of true private choice rather than an impermissible union of church and state. The decision was hailed as a great triumph by voucher proponents.

Beginning Legal Research

The goal of Point/Counterpoint is not only to provide the reader with an introduction to a controversial issue affecting society, but also to encourage the reader to explore the issue more fully. This appendix, then, is meant to serve as a guide to the reader in researching the current state of the law as well as exploring some of the public-policy arguments as to why existing laws should be changed or new laws are needed.

Like many types of research, legal research has become much faster and more accessible with the invention of the Internet. This appendix discusses some of the best starting points, but of course "surfing the Net" will uncover endless additional sources of information—some more reliable than others. Some important sources of law are not yet available on the Internet, but these can generally be found at the larger public and university libraries. Librarians usually are happy to point patrons in the right direction.

The most important source of law in the United States is the Constitution. Originally enacted in 1787, the Constitution outlines the structure of our federal government and sets limits on the types of laws that the federal government and state governments can pass. Through the centuries, a number of amendments have been added to or changed in the Constitution, most notably the first ten amendments, known collectively as the Bill of Rights, which guarantee important civil liberties. Each state also has its own constitution, many of which are similar to the U.S. Constitution. It is important to be familiar with the U.S. Constitution because so many of our laws are affected by its requirements. State constitutions often provide protections of individual rights that are even stronger than those set forth in the U.S. Constitution.

Within the guidelines of the U.S. Constitution, Congress—both the House of Representatives and the Senate—passes bills that are either vetoed or signed into law by the president. After the passage of the law, it becomes part of the United States Code, which is the official compilation of federal laws. The state legislatures use a similar process, in which bills become law when signed by the state's governor. Each state has its own official set of laws, some of which are published by the state and some of which are published by commercial publishers. The U.S. Code and the state codes are an important source of legal research; generally, legislators make efforts to make the language of the law as clear as possible.

However, reading the text of a federal or state law generally provides only part of the picture. In the American system of government, after the legislature passes laws and the executive (U.S. president or state governor) signs them, it is up to the judicial branch of the government, the court system, to interpret the laws and decide whether they violate any provision of the Constitution. At the state level, each state's supreme court has the ultimate authority in determining what a law means and whether or not it violates the state constitution. However, the federal courts—headed by the U.S. Supreme Court—can review state laws and court decisions to determine whether they violate federal laws or the U.S. Constitution. For example, a state court may find that a particular criminal law is valid under the state's constitution, but a federal court may then review the state court's decision and determine that the law is invalid under the U.S. Constitution.

It is important, then, to read court decisions when doing legal research. The Constitution uses language that is intentionally very general—for example, prohibiting "unreasonable searches and seizures" by the police—and court cases often provide more guidance. For example, the U.S. Supreme Court's 2001 decision in *Kyllo v. United States* held that scanning the outside of a person's house using a heat sensor to determine whether the person is growing marijuana is unreasonable—*if* it is done without a search warrant secured from a judge. Supreme Court decisions provide the most definitive explanation of the law of the land, and it is therefore important to include these in research. Often, when the Supreme Court has not decided a case on a particular issue, a decision by a federal appeals court or a state supreme court can provide guidance; but just as laws and constitutions can vary from state to state, so can federal courts be split on a particular interpretation of federal law or the U.S. Constitution. For example, federal appeals courts in Louisiana and California may reach opposite conclusions in similar cases.

Lawyers and courts refer to statutes and court decisions through a formal system of citations. Use of these citations reveals which court made the decision (or which legislature passed the statute) and when and enables the reader to locate the statute or court case quickly in a law library. For example, the legendary Supreme Court case *Brown v. Board of Education* has the legal citation 347 U.S. 483 (1954). At a law library, this 1954 decision can be found on page 483 of volume 347 of the U.S. Reports, the official collection of the Supreme Court's decisions. Citations can also be helpful in locating court cases on the Internet.

Understanding the current state of the law leads only to a partial under-standing of the issues covered by the POINT/COUNTERPOINT series. For a fuller understanding of the issues, it is necessary to look at public-policy arguments that the current state of the law is not adequately addressing the issue.

Many groups lobby for new legislation or changes to existing legislation; the National Rifle Association (NRA), for example, lobbies Congress and the state legislatures constantly to make existing gun control laws less restrictive and not to pass additional laws. The NRA and other groups dedicated to various causes might also intervene in pending court cases: a group such as Planned Parenthood might file a brief amicus curiae (as "a friend of the court")—called an "amicus brief"—in a lawsuit that could affect abortion rights. Interest groups also use the media to influence public opinion, issuing press releases and frequently appearing in interviews on news programs and talk shows. The books in POINT/COUNTERPOINT list some of the interest groups that are active in the issue at hand, but in each case there are countless other groups working at the local, state, and national levels. It is important to read everything with a critical eye, for sometimes interest groups present information in a way that can be read only to their advantage. The informed reader must always look for bias.

Finding sources of legal information on the Internet is relatively simple thanks to "portal" sites such as FindLaw (*www.findlaw.com*), which provides access to a variety of constitutions, statutes, court opinions, law review articles, news articles, and other resources—including all Supreme Court decisions issued since 1893. Other useful sources of information include the U.S. Government Printing Office (*www.gpo.gov*), which contains a complete copy of the U.S. Code, and the Library of Congress's THOMAS system (*thomas.loc.gov*), which offers access to bills pending before Congress as well as recently passed laws. Of course, the Internet changes every second of every day, so it is best to do some independent searching. Most cases, studies, and opinions that are cited or referred to in public debate can be found online—and *everything* can be found in one library or another.

The Internet can provide a basic understanding of most important legal issues, but not all sources can be found there. To find some documents it is necessary to visit the law library of a university or a public law library; some cities have public law libraries, and many library systems keep legal documents at the main branch. On the following page are some common citation forms.

COMMON CITATION FORMS

Source of Law	Sample Citation	Notes
U.S. Supreme Court	*Employment Division* v. *Smith*, 485 U.S. 660 (1988)	The U.S. Reports is the official record of Supreme Court decisions. There is also an unofficial Supreme Court ("S. Ct.") reporter.
U.S. Court of Appeals	*United States* v. *Lambert*, 695 F.2d 536 (11th Cir.1983)	Appellate cases appear in the Federal Reporter, designated by "F." The 11th Circuit has jurisdiction in Alabama, Florida, and Georgia.
U.S. District Court	*Carillon Importers, Ltd.* v. *Frank Pesce Group, Inc.*, 913 F.Supp. 1559 (S.D.Fla.1996)	Federal trial-level decisions are reported in the Federal Supplement ("F. Supp."). Some states have multiple federal districts; this case originated in the Southern District of Florida.
U.S. Code	Thomas Jefferson Commemoration Commission Act, 36 U.S.C., §149 (2002)	Sometimes the popular names of legislation—names with which the public may be familiar—are included with the U.S. Code citation.
State Supreme Court	*Sterling* v. *Cupp*, 290 Ore. 611, 614, 625 P.2d 123, 126 (1981)	The Oregon Supreme Court decision is reported in both the state's reporter and the Pacific regional reporter.
State Statute	Pennsylvania Abortion Control Act of 1982, 18 Pa. Cons. Stat. 3203-3220 (1990)	States use many different citation formats for their statutes.

DAVID L. HUDSON, JR., is an author-attorney who has published widely on First Amendment and other constitutional law issues. Hudson is a research attorney with the First Amendment Center at Vanderbilt University and a First Amendment contributing editor to the American Bar Association's *Preview of the United States Supreme Court Cases*. He obtained his undergraduate degree from Duke University and his law degree from Vanderbilt University Law School.

ALAN MARZILLI, M.A., J.D., lives in Washington, D.C., and is a program associate with Advocates for Human Potential, Inc., a research and consulting firm based in Sudbury, Mass., and Albany, N.Y. He primarily works on developing training and educational materials for agencies of the federal government on topics such as housing, mental health policy, employment, and transportation. He has spoken on mental health issues in 30 states, the District of Columbia, and Puerto Rico; his work has included training mental health administrators, nonprofit management and staff, and people with mental illnesses and their families on a wide variety of topics, including effective advocacy, community-based mental health services, and housing. He has written several handbooks and training curricula that are used nationally and as far away as the territory of Guam. He managed statewide and national mental health advocacy programs and worked for several public interest lobbying organizations while studying law at Georgetown University. He has written more than a dozen books, including numerous titles in the POINT/COUNTERPOINT series.